A GRAMMAR
SCHOOL GIRL

The first day in our new house, June 1968.

A GRAMMAR SCHOOL GIRL

Life and Education in
Birmingham 1968–1975

Grace Caroline Holte

BREWIN BOOKS

BREWIN BOOKS
19 Enfield Ind. Estate,
Redditch,
Worcestershire,
B97 6BY
www.brewinbooks.com

Published by Brewin Books 2023

A CIP catalogue record for this book is
available from the British Library.

ISBN: 978-1-85858-754-7

Printed and bound in Great Britain
by 4edge Ltd.

Contents

IN MEMORY OF ANDREW CLIVE ATKINS

Dear Friend and 'Little Brother'

1960–2020

And also The Twenty-One

1974

www.bbc.co.uk/news/uk-england-birmingham-47375087
Who They Were

Dramatis Personae

Family

Dad (Bill), Mom (Lily) and Grace and Susie
Nan (Elsie)
Uncle Bill, Auntie Margaret and Mark and Matthew
Auntie Floss, Uncle Bert and David and Mark
Great Uncle Fred, Great Aunt Min, and Gill and Hazel
Uncle John, Auntie Carol and Jason
Auntie Eileen and Dean and Tracey
Uncle Charlie, Auntie Ann and Marie
Sarah the Dog

Dad's brother Uncle Albert, Auntie Mary, Jim and Janet
Uncle Charlie, Auntie Lil, step cousins Eileen and Margaret and cousin John
Uncle Ray, Auntie Jean (Dad's sister) and Paul and Zara

Neighbours

Kim Harrison, and her parents Jean and Les
Julie Lane, brother Peter and her parents
Maureen and Brian Caldicott and daughter Kim
Jack and Frances and their daughter, Shirley and their two sons
Jackie and Jen, the twins

On the Estate

Dr Carolan at the Newtown Health Centre
Reverend Geoffrey Brown, St George's Church, and his curate, the Rev John Cox

Friends

Johnnie Murray, Dad's right hand man at Tucker Fasteners, wife Maureen, and children Ann-Marie and Paul
Stan and Barbara Atkins, Lynne, Andrew and Joanne
John and Pat Bowman
Frank and Elsie Collins, Marie and Vanessa
Johnnie and Nora Niven and young John
Harold and Clare Styles, young Harold and Susan
Jim and Phil Grogan
Roy and Doreen McManus, Lisa and Helen

School

Miss Reid and Miss Sargeant, Headmistresses
Miss Boggis (Latin), Deputy Head
Mrs Wax (French), Miss Tolley (English), Mrs Tunstall (English), Mrs Davies (English), Mrs Gough (English), Mrs Adie (French), Mrs Gregory (English), Mrs Geoghegan (Music), Miss James (English), Miss Hood (Maths), Miss Naish (Maths), Miss Allen later Mrs Dolman (French), Mr Dolman (RE), Mr Aldridge (French), Mr Arnold (RE), Miss Mold and Mrs Craddock (PE), Mr Billington (Music), Miss Beechill (Science), Mrs Eagleton (Biology), Mr Clark (Chemistry), Mr Hutchinson (Physics), Miss Hinton/Mrs Fletcher (Geography), Mrs Garrett (Cookery), Miss Stock (Needlework), Mrs Thorne (History), Mrs Wragge (Physics) and Miss Ewoldt (Biology)
Mr Wilcox (Porter)
Lower School friends: Jennie Barrett, Lesley Miller, Margaret McLaney, Yvonne Osborne and Janice Brandreth
Sixth Form friends: Lorna Hitchin, Jill Turner, Pat Ruston, Janet Buet, Yvonne Jackson and Kerry Cusack
The girls of IIIZ, Lower IVZ, Upper IVZ, Lower VZ, Upper VZ 1968–1973
The girls of the Lower and Upper Sixth, 1973–1975

Introduction

In 2018, I published my memoir *The Girl from Guildford Street*, a memoir of growing up in a working class area of Birmingham, in the back to backs, in the 1960s, a decade of great hope and promise. It ended in 1968, when we left the back to backs, which were about to be demolished, for one of the new council estates which were then being built as Birmingham was being redeveloped. This was followed by my novel *Tales of Guildford Street* (2020), published under the name Emilia Williams, a novel of family life in the back to backs between the 1920s to 1960s.

Both books met with a very warm reception. I was privileged to be able to visit lots of groups and libraries to do book talks in which many people came along to tell me how the books had reflected their own experience. One of the requests I had was "Can you write the story of Birmingham in the 1970s?"

I had never thought of doing this. The 1960s were a time of great personal happiness for me and my family, who were all alive and healthy, and active in politics and Trade Unionism. We were surrounded by the beautiful red brick buildings of Civic Victorian Birmingham. The decade saw a great deal of progressive political progress, and events such as the World Cup victory of 1966 and the moon landings. Birmingham was a centre of trade and industry, The Workshop of the World, The City of a Thousand and One Trades, and had almost full employment, which meant that working class people were able to enjoy benefits such as car ownership. The decade ended with a bang with the Equal Pay for Women Act (1970), a cause for which my mother had campaigned.

In contrast the Birmingham of the 1970s was a sadder place. The red brick disappeared, to be replaced by grey stone and concrete, and the new council estates with high rises and maisonettes. Houses, shops, churches, cinemas, libraries and colleges went under the bulldozer. Old communities were replaced by new council estates. The decade was marked by change and conflict, strikes and strife. There were cataclysmic events such as the Birmingham Bombings of 1974. It was a sad decade for my family too, which for the first time knew death, divorce, illness, separation and depression.

It struck me that the sadder story of my family during this time, in fact, mirrored Birmingham's experience; it was a greyer, sadder decade. But for me, as a teenager, there were also happier times, such as discovering the City Centre. And there were all the new material advantages such as washing machines, colour TVs, fridges, telephones and hair dryers. I decided that it was a story worth writing and that Birmingham still came out of this sad decade with her indomitable spirit unbeaten.

Thanks are due to Brewin Books, who published my books; they are the foremost publishers of Midlands history, a story that deserves to be told.

I

First Days in the New House

1968–1969

As Dad and I draw up in our tank of a car, the A60 Cambridge, which has replaced our faithful A40 Farina, my mom is standing at the door of 426 New John Street West, our new home on the Newtown Estate, and beaming.

Movers are busy with our humble sticks of furniture, but Mom has already hung up the net curtains from the old house "so that no-one can see in!" All of the furniture has come from Guildford Street; the rent is going up from fifteen shillings a week to £5, and there's no spare money.

It's a warm June day and the world seems full of hope. "Let's take a photo of them," shrieks Mom, brandishing the Box Brownie which Dad acquired in the Marines, already second-hand, but which has photographed our family for the last twenty years. My sister and I are still dressed alike (my mother thinks it is 'sweet') and today we are wearing matching shorts and tops, and sandals. We pose patiently outside the new front window, and then we tear off to explore the new house.

The house, like the Newtown Estate, is brand new. To make way for the new council estates of the 1970s, the old council stock mainly back to backs and terraced housing dating from the Victorian era, is being demolished. Ours is one of a row of six, facing New John Street West. Behind us are the streets and cul de sacs (new words for us; previously they were known as 'courts'), and the brand new tower blocks of the Estate: Thornton House, Fallows House and Weston House.

It's a beautiful day, and we run all over the house. Ours is an end of row, so we have a side wall, backing onto a piece of grass with a discouraging sign, *Keep Off The Grass. Ball Games Disallowed.* Not like Guildford Street, where the lads played football in the street. There is a garden at the back and front of the house. Two gardens! We have only ever had a shared backyard! Sadly, at present the gardens are not very exciting. They are full of dirt, stones and rubble. The front one has a low iron rail around it, and the back, a fence of what looks like chicken wire.

"We can't play there," says Susie, shuddering.

"I'll soon turn them both into a real garden, with trees and flowers," promises Dad.

Our new house has a real porch; before, we have entered straight into the living room. In fact, we now have three rooms downstairs, a kitchen, living room, and small dining room, which have large windows looking out onto the gardens. All of the kitchen is fitted with cupboards. The houses we live in might look exactly the same, but the council is going to ensure that they are fit for living in. They have done us proud.

A flight of stairs takes us up to three bedrooms, one much smaller than the other two, and a bathroom and toilet! Dad has already discovered the boiler in an airing cupboard and turned it on. We marvel as we turn on the taps, and steaming hot water gushes from every tap in the house. "No more tin baths in front of the fire, no more public washing baths," sings Susie.

There are no radiators in the house – it is tiled throughout with dark brown tiles, and when Dad throws another switch in the cupboard under the stairs, where the gas meter is, and instantly, the tiles begin to heat up. We have underfloor central heating. Instantly, Dad turns them off – it is a hot day.

Yes, the council has done us proud. They are building thousands of homes on new estates all over Birmingham, and they might all be little boxes that look the same, as in the song on the radio, but they are boxes fit for Brummies to live in.

What is going into the new house unfortunately doesn't quite fit.

The rent, collected by Mr Ballinger on a fortnightly basis in Guildford Street, was thirty shillings. It is now going up to five pounds a week, and my dad has to pay it with his brand new account. He opened it when he was promoted to foreman at Tucker Fasteners, and his best mate Johnnie Murray is going to be his chargehand. Dad went to Lloyd's in Birmingham on the Queensway to open his bank account because they are open on Saturday mornings. He works Monday to Friday.

However, despite the bank account and cheque book (there are of course no speed banks yet), we can't afford to buy any new furniture at all, so everything from Guildford Street has to be fitted into New John Street West. And this is a problem. The old gas cooker was left behind as we have a new electric cooker, which Mom experiments with.

The old cabinet goes into the kitchen, and a drop leaf table and four chairs, hastily purchased from The House that Jack Built on the Newtown Row. We don't have a dining table and chairs as we have never had a dining room. Previously, we ate off a green baize card table, which hung on the wall from a nail. Now that goes into the electricity meter cupboard under the stairs.

It doesn't matter that we have only a kitchen cabinet, because Mom has a whole fitted kitchen of cupboards, whereas before she had the trapdoor over the cellar, and a sink with cold running water. There is a three bar fire in the living room, which Dad is testing out along with the underfloor heating. "No more coal, and it's a good thing you two don't believe in Father Christmas anymore, because that means no chimneys," he says, laughing. This makes me think. Until now, we have had a coal delivery every Friday, unchaining the grate at the front of the house for the coalmen, and the necessary monthly visit from the chimney sweep with his brushes. What will they do if we don't use them?

Susie and I pelt upstairs, to check the bedrooms. The bathroom, decorated in beige, is tiny, but it is a bathroom! And we have a toilet! No more chamber pots, no more outside toilets with spiders and daddy long legs running rampant!

More to our interest are the three bedrooms, two large and one small. I set my heart on the small one, as it has a view onto the back garden, but Dad says we had better share until we "get used to the new house". Susie and I scowl. Our two beds, with their candlewick spreads, are moved easily up the stairs; at 37 Guildford Street, they had to take the windows out because the stairs were almost vertical, and twisted.

We have our old wardrobes, and a dressing table. Susie has a box for her jigsaws, and Dad has a surprise for me: a little white bookcase, purchased from The House that Jack Built, for my growing book collection. Thinking that we have grown out of them, we sadly relegate our dolls and teddies to the wardrobe, along with the farmyard set, the dolls' house and our electric train set. As yet, we are not ready to part with them.

Mom and Dad also have their double bed, wardrobe and dressing table. This is quite easy. It's not so easy downstairs. Our three-piece suite, a green sofa and two chairs looks lost in the huge living room. The sofa stands in the middle of the wall, opposite the three bar electric fire, and a chair under each large window. The only carpet halfway big enough for the living room, or the right shape, is that green one that was in the living room at Guildford Street, and even so, there is a strip of brown tiled floor at each end of the room where it falls short. As for the bedrooms, they have whatever carpet was left, and Dad cuts it down with a Swiss knife, but mainly, there's gaps round the edges. All of our rugs go into the dining room and kitchen.

Our twelve inch black and white telly sits forlornly on a small table in the living room. We are going to have to sit really close to it to see the picture, and Dad is fiddling around with the aerial to try and get one. The entire house is painted a pale shade which Dad says is called magnolia, but which looks a dreary beige to me, and I already miss our nursery rhyme wallpaper, and the living room, yellow with chocolate roses. But Dad says cheerfully he will paper the new house throughout, once he gets to Dulux.

Susie nudges me. "Let's go out and explore, they're busy," she whispers. We quietly make our way out of the front door. The movers are all gone now, and Dad tipped them ten shillings. We didn't have to pay them, the council does, because we were forcibly moved.

A girl about Susie's age is standing at the end of our drive. She is tall and slim, with curly blond hair, and like us dressed in shorts and a shirt. "I'm Kim Harrison," she says, "I live at the other end." Over the next few days, Kim is our guide to the delights of the Newtown Estate.

The Newtown Estate is brand new, and it stands bordered by Newtown Row, Summer Lane, and the brand new Newtown Precinct where the Outer Circle no 11 bus stops. Three tower blocks dominate its skyline: Thornton House, Fallows House where Nan is going to live, and Weston House. Towering over the new precinct is the double tower block Inkerman House.

Our street faces straight out onto New John Street West, but it is a busy road, and to park in the car park at the back of our house, Dad enters via Attenborough Close on Summer Lane. There is a new pub here called The Lamplighter, but Dad says he will take Uncle Albert when he comes round, to the Clements Arms on Newtown Row, a tiny Victorian pub which isn't as grand as the Bartons Arms.

"We're at no 418," says Kim. Despite the numbers, there are now only nine houses on New John Street West. The rest were terraced back to backs, like ours, and have been demolished; 417 houses no longer exist.

Our playground up till now has been the street or the back yard, but until the gardens have been done up, we have nowhere. All of the flats have concrete playgrounds outside with a slide, a climbing frame and some rather oddly shaped artefacts which don't seem to be anything at all. They resemble sputniks.

Still, the estate, bordered by Newtown Row and Summer Lane is a wonder to the three of us. It's a new world, the council estates of 1970s Birmingham.

When we have finished exploring, we head back to the house. The gardens, we can see, are not yet fit for us to play in as they are full of rubble and rubbish, back and front, the front being bordered with a white iron rail, and the back with wire netting. The grass next to the house bears the sign: *Do Not Play on the Grass, by order of Birmingham City Council.* The roads surrounding the estate are all very busy, and I realise that the lads will never again play football in the street, as they used to in Guildford Street.

Tea is egg and chips around the new table, with Mom coming to grips with the new electric stove, and then we peer at the twelve inch black and white telly the whole length of the living room. Bed in an unfamiliar room is strange, so maybe Dad was right after all.

Over the next few days, we find out more about the Newtown Estate. Mom takes us shopping down to the new precinct; like everything that is being built now, it is all in concrete and is extremely ugly. However, the shops are wonderful, so we don't mind. It has a post office, where Mom can collect her Family Allowance every Monday, it has banks, it has supermarkets, shoe shops, bakers, butchers, two modern pubs called The Paddock and The Griffin, furniture shop, grocers, and a newsagent (but Mom intends to remain faithful to Cooper's Newsagent on Newtown Row). Again, we spare a thought for our old haunt, the Lozells Road, but we have just discovered a wonderful round (concrete) market in the middle of the precinct. It is made up of what seems to be hundreds of tiny stalls. While Mom is looking at some carpet samples at one of them, we discover a toy and book stall. I find straight away a stand of paperback books, mainly Armada, with some of my new favourites: Monica Edwards, Malcolm Saville and the Chalet School. I resolve to break open the post box money box I share with Susie. And Dillon's has a splendid array of sweets and chocolate: Dairy Box and Black Magic for Mother's Day and Christmas, and Opal Fruits, Spangles, Refreshers and Lovehearts for us. And a bar of Old Jamaica for Dad on Father's Day.

Of course, Mom will still need to shop every day because we don't get a fridge freezer till much later. The only frozen food she gets are Birds Eye Fish Fingers, and the occasional pack of frozen peas at the weekend. Our shopping needs are still very simple: there are, for example, only two brands of crisps, Smiths and Golden Wonder. What you buy, you eat.

We walk round to the back of the precinct, where we find a brand new building called the Newtown Community Centre. We read the *What's On* outside: all sorts of things for all ages! "I want to go to that," I say, pointing at the Hazeltree School of Dance, every Wednesday night. I am eleven years old and have never danced a step. But all the books about ballet which I borrow from the library are about poor girls who have never danced a step, then they start ballet lessons and somebody discovers they are a genius, and they end up at the Royal School of Ballet.

We peer into the new swimming baths next door. A long, shimmering blue pool, a café, and a spectators' gallery; we can't wait to go! "The Newtown Estate is lovely," says Susie as we walk back to the new house.

Our week is spent with Kim, cycling and roller skating all over the estate, and the sun shines every day. The estate has something in common with Guildford Street; it has not a blade of grass, the few areas of grass there are outside the high rise flats warn us that we cannot play on them. Everything is concrete.

Mom has a solution to our curtainless problem. She has found some cheap net for sale in the market; they cut it for her to the lengths of our windows and Dad fixes them up with curtain wire so at least people can't see in the window. But our carpets still are too small for the floors and our old furniture looks shabby in the big new house.

Dad is busy drawing up plans for his two gardens. He will have to do it all himself, dig it all up and plant flowers and trees. The truth is, as the rent has gone up from fifteen shillings to five pounds a week, there is not much they can afford at present, even though Dad is now foreman at work, and Johnnie Murray is chargehand. And Mom still walks straight up New John Street West four nights a week to Lucas's Great King Street, now housed in the middle of a grassy space paid for by Lucas's and known as Lucas's Park, although it has no park features in it, and we are not impressed. It does, however, have a brand new church and next to the church are two houses for our beloved vicar Mr Geoffrey Brown, who used to visit William Cowper with his guitar, and his curate John Cox.

We read the church noticeboard. There is a youth club, Tuesdays and Thursdays, called Seekers which we might come to. I have finished Brownies at the Settlement now and am not going on to Guides, and Susie won't go if I don't. There is also a poster about something called the Newtown Bonanza, a celebration of the Newtown Estate, and a jumble sale at the Settlement.

Mr Brown turns up, guitar slung over his shoulder and greets us cheerfully. "I'm starting a newspaper, called the *Newtown News*," he says, "a paper for the whole estate. To bring us together. I want the first Miss Newtown to deliver the paper to a house. Would your mum and dad mind?" Mind! They'd be ecstatic! "And we'll be in a paper," breathes Susie. "I'll call in and see them then," he says, which of course he will have to do as we do not have a phone. Nobody has a phone.

Nan is moving into Fallows House on Saturday and we have really missed her. We haven't seen her all week, as we don't want to go round to Guildford Street, we don't want to see the old house boarded up. As with us, the Council have arranged for the removal of her furniture, as we have all been forcibly rehoused. This is because Shelter said Birmingham's council housing was the worst in the country; that was after *Cathy Come Home* was shown on the telly. So now they are re-housing us as fast as they can, and they have to get a lot of people into a small space. Just like the back to backs we have just left. And the answer is the high rise flats which are going up all over Newtown; sixteen altogether, including Inkerman House, the biggest in the UK.

It is all very *concrete*. It is all very *grey*. I have grown up on a street of mellow red Victorian brick. But the Newtown Estate has one thing in common with Guildford Street; there are no flowers, or trees, or a blade of grass. But we do now have gardens, even if they consist of dirt, stone and rubble.

Nan's Council moving van turns up on the Saturday morning at Fallows House. Her third floor flat is right above the sign and after seeing her furniture moved in, she walks around clutching her keys to the new flat. We are waiting. Now the movers have problems. When they moved our stuff, they took all the windows out to get the beds, wardrobes and sofas out, sliding them down ladders. The staircases in the back to backs were narrow and almost vertical. "Health and safety is running wild," observe my parents, shop stewards. But you can't do this in a thirteen floor block of flats. Luckily, the stairs are very, very wide. So the movers have to stagger up the stairs with all the furniture.

The high rise flats have a bad name now, but in the 1960s, they were seen as a great solution for housing a lot of elderly people in a small space. And Nan, who has lived in a back to back without a toilet or bathroom or hot running water or proper heating for nearly forty years, is delighted.

No 9 Fallows House has a bedroom, a bathroom, a living room and a kitchen. Every room faces out, and it is full of light. Like our house, it is painted magnolia throughout, and the floor is brown tiling. And best of all, it has a little door that leads onto a balcony, where Nan will be able to sit and enjoy her view of the estate. Like our house, her carpets and curtains don't fit. "I'll soon sort out the curtains," says Mom confidently. The furniture looks shabby as well – I think it is the same furniture that she has had since she got married in 1930. A sofa, on which all of the family have sat, a chair, a bed, a wardrobe, a radio, a twelve inch black and white telly, a kitchen table and four chairs have to be dispersed around the flat.

But Nan thinks it is lovely, and she makes us a pot of tea. She lowers her voice; "I've got something sad to tell you." Ever since we can remember, my sister and I have wanted a pet. My Nan, resignedly, has been through a series of cats and dogs that belonged to my mom and Uncle Bill – all rescue animals. Uncle John kept pigeons in a shed in the back yard – Susie and I went in to feed them every day, with bags of corn. We want a pet so much that we capture two caterpillars, called Peppy and Stripey, put them in a plastic washing up bowl, and lovingly feed them on grass for a week, after which they die, and we consign their corpses to a patch of grass in the yard with many a bitter tear.

Then there is Nan's goldfish – known simply as The Goldfish – given to her by the rag and bone man in a plastic bag, only supposed to survive for a week, and now over 20 and going strong. He lives in a half bowl which my uncle affixed to the wall, and pops his head out of the water when he sees anyone coming with fish food. Dad is just now fixing it on the wall in the flat.

About a year ago, Susie and I 'adopted' a dog on Guildford Street. He belonged to a man who owns a wholesale yard and he calls him Thinny, and like so many others, the dog wanders the street all day. He pitches up in our yard, where Susie and I make a big fuss of him and Mom feeds him, because he looks so thin. We call him Skipper.

Soon he is sitting on our doorstep every morning, waiting to come in, and Mom lets him stay on Saturday night, when he curls up contentedly in front of our fire.

Nan lowers her voice, "He has been on your doorstep *every morning*," she says. "Just waiting. I fed him." Susie and I look at each other, appalled. Our eyes fill with tears. Dad looks resigned. "That's it," he says. "I'll go round and make an offer." And indeed later that afternoon, he returns with Skipper on a lead. My mom runs down to the precinct for dog food, Dad resignedly puts aside the seven and sixpence for the dog licence, and Susie and I have a dog. "I got taken for thirty shillings," says Dad bitterly. He goes off to the Newtown Post Office for a dog licence.

We get to know all our new neighbours. Next door to us are the Pickerings, Jack and Frances, with their daughter Shirley and her two brothers. Julie Lane lives with her parents and brother Peter, and she goes with me to the School of Dance. There are the twins, Jackie and Jen, who live with their parents and are exactly alike. Kim Harrison lives at the top of the row with Jean and Les, her mom and dad. Kim Caldicott lives in the maisonettes with Brian and Maureen, and Mrs Busby beams down on us from Thornton House and throws down bones for Skipper. We are close knit neighbours and within a few years our gardens, which began as derelict patches of rubble, are winning the Birmingham's Best Kept Gardens Competition.

Over the long summer holidays, when the sun seems to shine every day, Mom has to start thinking about my school uniform for King Edward's, Handsworth. We have already been to Open Day at school, where she has ordered a navy blue leotard for Dance, and a black swimming costume with the school badge. Now she has received a list as long as my arm. Of course, they have been saving in the Post Office for years and they have their money, but still it is a financial strain, especially now that the rent has gone up from fifteen shillings a week to five pounds (paid from Dad's brand new bank account, Lloyd's in the precinct; the council rent collector has retired and hung up his bag for good).

We take stock. I have in fact a tennis racket; it was my last Christmas present from my last Lucas's Christmas party, "Thank God I don't need to be an Auntie anymore," says Mom. Dad's manager at work has a daughter at King Edward's and he generously donates her old hockey stick and boots; they are a bit big for me and remind Dad of his experience of *Birmingham Evening Mail* charity boots in the 1930s (they were always too big).

But everything else must be bought. One bright Saturday morning in July, we head off to Birmingham on the No 7 bus down Summer Lane, armed with shopping bags and The List. Susie is left in Dad's care, because Mom doesn't want her to see the clothes she will be wearing in two years' time; they are happily ensconced in front of *Grandstand*. Susie has got a bit of a thing about Hand Me Downs, even though our clothes are always immaculate.

First stop is Horne Brothers and School Fashions, where the majority of the uniform is to be bought. It is all navy blue and bottle green, which I think is so ugly, not like the pretty colours they wear in my Chalet School books. I have a pinafore dress, two light blue shirts, a striped tie which Mom says Dad will show me how to tie with a Windsor knot, and a King Edward's navy blue pullover. The King Edward's blazer costs more than the rest of the items put together. I have to have a rather odd purse, again navy blue, felt with the school arms on it and attached to a piece of blue cord. "To wear over your shoulder and stop you from losing it I suppose," says Mom, staring at it doubtfully. And it will of course contain my dinner money and bus fare. Mom hands over the cash, sighing a bit at handing over money for what seem to be very ugly items.

Then it's off to Harry Parkes sports shop, which is exciting, as he used to be an Aston Villa player and he might be there. He isn't, but there are lots of black and white photos of his glory days. Here we purchase blue and green socks for hockey, a light blue aertex shirt, and a wrap over navy blue skirt. "You might be a bit cold in the winter," says Mom doubtfully. But I am dreaming of hockey, netball, tennis and rounders.

Finally, to Grey's Department Store because she is running out of money, but she thinks King Edward's is a cut above the Co-op, she finds a navy blue mac for winter wear. It is *enormous*. Although we are now laden down with bags, as a special treat, Mom allows me to ride up and down the escalators at Lewis's, and then it's over to the Midland Educational, where I spend a happy half a crown on a Ruby Ferguson. Then to Bull Street, to catch the bus home not to Summer Lane but Newtown Row. Saturday night fish and chips.

2

First Days in the New School

1968–1969

The holidays fly past, and I am due to start at King Edward's Grammar School on Thursday September 5th. "I'm coming with you," announces Mom. "Susie can go over to Nan's, and go to school from there." Susie brightens at this; we love Nan's flat. And she is heading, like me, for two years in Top Class, working on Eleven Plus papers, though they say the Eleven Plus is finishing and all our schools are going comprehensive. "Not before Susie gets into King Edward's though," says Dad confidently.

I awake with a sinking feeling. I am also awakened early. Very early. Up till now, we have had a ten minute walk to school; now I have to catch two buses. I clamber wearily into my new school uniform all of which is too big and also, despite being brand new, very ugly. In fact, the Newtown Estate despite being brand new, is also very ugly. This is now my life.

September also marks the beginning of porridge for breakfast, and Liberty bodices, as Mom thinks we feel the cold. We read the *Daily Mirror* over breakfast, delivered by Cooper's Newsagent's on Newtown Row, who have always delivered our papers. The paper boy has a word with Mom. "Cooper's is going," she says, "he's moving. They're knocking down most of Newtown Row. I'll have to pop in and say goodbye. I'll ask Dillon's in the precinct to do the papers." Susie's and my eyes meet; we have a huge roll of comics every week from Cooper's: *Bunty, Diana, June and School Friend, Mandy.* Dad has been saying for years they are a waste of money; this might be his opportunity to cancel them!

After breakfast I put on my huge navy blue mac, and Mom anxiously pins back the sleeves. Susie, in her new red winter coat from the Co-op with its fur collar, giggles hysterically at the hem of my mac sweeping the floor. I shoulder my satchel with my new pencil case, and seeing myself in the mirror in the hall, reflect that Malory Towers this ain't.

Nan is looking out from her balcony, and with a triumphant flick of her blonde ponytail with its red ribbon, Susie takes the lift two floors up. I think of Mom walking to meet her at dinner time, and their lonely lunch together, and I won't be there. Mom and I continue past Fallows House, over a patch of grass to Newtown Row. The only building now standing on this side of the road is the *Sportsman*, a pub which looks odd as there is nothing surrounding it.

The cheerful looking No 33 bus takes us up to Six Ways, where we cross the underpass for the 40E bus stop at the bottom of Lozells Road. It stops right where the old sign for Guildford Street is affixed to Gower Street School, where it meets the Lozells Road. I have tears in my eyes for a minute looking at it, and thinking of the house. It is no longer there, it was demolished over the summer, and there is nothing left now of it but a patch of waste ground. And Mom has just said Newtown Row is to be demolished. The old Birmingham changeth, giving way to the new, and it's not pretty.

There are a few moments of anxiety as the 40E is late. "It has a very long route, the E stands for Extra – it's for workers," explains Mom. The 40E eventually turns up. Like the 33, it is one of Birmingham's new buses, the same blue and cream livery, but instead of a double decker with a rear open platform and a driver and conductor, you enter at the front, the doors are automatic, and there is a driver/conductor. Mom doesn't care too much for this, as you need the right fare, and I miss the conductor's little silver ticket machine. "Not a good idea," says Mom, the shop steward, as we sit down upstairs in the front seat at my request, "because it means one job where there used to be two. And lots of the clippies were women, it takes their jobs away."

I am busy staring at the Lozells Road, where Mom used to shop every Saturday. Half the shops are closed down and boarded up, and the Villa Cross Picture House, where we saw many films, looks forlorn and neglected. We get off where Villa Road meets Soho Road, and walk up to the fine red brick building. Mom clears her throat, "I'll be back at four o' clock..." Her voice trails off. She bends down and gives me a peck on the cheek, turns round, and walks off. I stare after her. Then I shoulder my satchel, and join the hundreds of girls dressed in navy blue uniform flooding through the front gates.

I really have no idea what I am supposed to do next, do I go up to anybody and say, "I'm new?" A lady in a smart two-piece suit is standing at the door. She has neatly set brown hair, thick horn-rimmed glasses, and she holds a clipboard. She sees me looking lost.

"All new girls over here," she calls.

"I'm Mrs Wax," she says kindly. "Who are you?"

"Grace Caroline Holte." My voice comes out as a squeak.

"That's nice, because I'm your new form mistress. You'll be in 3Z." She smiles.

Three other mistresses are standing round, and we are separated into four groups. I trail off after Mrs Wax, down a long corridor, down the stairs into a long room on the ground floor. It is full of racks with pegs attached, and we have to hang up our brand new navy blue macs. Our 'turkey red' shoe bags are also hung up here. We take off our outdoor shoes, and replace them with our indoor shoes. Dad has lettered my name on the outside of my bag in black ink, and Mom has sewn personal name tapes onto everything else.

Down the stairs and into a classroom with high windows, a chalkboard and a desk and chair at the front, and four rows of desks and chairs, all equipped with an inkwell.

"Ladies, you are to sit alphabetically, till I know your names." Which means I am halfway down but at the back (which is good), but not near the window (which is bad). Thirty eleven year old girls, all dressed the same, look around and stare at each other.

"Assembly first, ladies, and then I'll give you your timetables." We are now ladies. The girl nearest the door, at her command, springs up and opens the door for Mrs Wax. One by one, we stand up and follow in a line down the corridor, into a central hall, and onto a designated row of chairs that a prefect guides us to. At William Cowper, we sat on the floor.

We all stand up with a huge shuffling of chairs as a tall thin lady mounts the platform at the front of the hall. I look around covertly at 1,000 girls (there were 50 at William Cowper altogether), steal a look at my Cinderella Timex wristwatch, a Christmas gift, and sigh. It is only nine o'clock and already everything is so new and strange.

Miss Reid welcomes us. She has the posh voice I remember, although she tells us she is Scottish. When not standing at the lectern, she seats herself on a regal wooden throne and beams as girls play the piano, or read the Lessons and the notices. Behind her is the coat of arms of the Tudors, flanked by two white cameos against the pale blue painted hall. Two portraits of Edward the Sixth hang on the wall.

We begin the day by singing *All Things Bright and Beautiful* from a little blue book called *Songs of Praise*, which was given to us in class. Then it's down on our knees for prayers and Our Father, and back on our chairs for Notices. I listen as a stream of notices about the hockey team, the library, the Head Girls and the prefects is read out, and it sounds just like St Clare's or the Chalet School.

After notices the teacher sitting at the fine grand piano launches enthusiastically into a lively march, and we leave the Hall class by class, with the Sixth Form leaving first. The Sixth Form do not wear school uniforms, and seem very sophisticated to my unworldly eyes.

Miss Reid, eagle-eyed, stands on the platform, watching. She wears a long black gown, as do some of the other teachers, which Mrs Wax has explained is a university gown. Nobody in my family has ever been to University. She beckons with her finger as I pass, "Come here, my dear." Crimson, I join her on the platform. Everybody looks sideways as they pass. When they are all gone, she gently touches the top of my head. "Your hair ribbon isn't school navy blue. Ask your mother to replace it."

I remember all the shopping Mom has done. I have grown my hair out of my Mary Quant bob in recent years, and she has dressed it in a ponytail, with the ribbon high on my head. With tears in my eyes, I make my way back to my classroom. I seem to have made a bad start.

We now have what is called a "double period" with Mrs Wax, which mainly consists of her taking in our dinner money, filling in a large blue register, and giving out the timetable. Monday to Friday 8.50am – 4pm, I have to be somewhere every hour of the day and unlike William Cowper, every lesson is in a different room: The Geography Room, The History Room, The Music Room, The Science Block (that sounds exciting!), The Needlework Room, The Cookery Room, The Gym, The Playing Fields and The Art Room.

Morning break is spent in a large, cold room known as the Playroom, after we line up in the corridors for iced buns and milk. I take mine dolefully into the Playroom, lean against a radiator and look around. A very pretty girl with brown hair and large brown eyes comes up.

"Aren't you in 3Z? I'm Lesley."

"Yes, I am," I say hopefully.

She eyes me up and down. "We'll be best friends," she announces, putting her arm through mine. My heart sings as we make our way back to Room 27. I have a friend!

At dinner time, Lesley introduces me to Jennie, in 3W. Jennie is a small, fair blonde. "We were at the same school," Jennie tells me as we queue up for dinner. "We go to tap dance together at my mom's School of Dance. I can't understand why we're not in the same class!"

I have already found out that most of the girls here come from Cherry Orchard or Rookery Road Schools. There is nobody from William Cowper, or our part of Birmingham and moreover, I have already found out that many of these girls support West Bromwich Albion! Birmingham City are the deadly rivals of AVFC, so I have only heard vaguely of the Albion, and hardly knew that they existed. This is another world!

There are three sittings for dinnertime, which is an hour and twenty minutes long and we are not allowed to leave the school premises. Ours is Third, announced with a bell ringing and we are starving. And what a let-down it is.

In these post Jamie Oliver days, it is difficult to remember how dreadful institutionalised food could be. To a certain extent the Council School Meals Department is trying to feed us nutritiously as every day is meat and two veg (but if you are a vegetarian, forget it). The problem for us is how it is cooked. Meat tends to be either burnt black or pink. Vegetables are boiled to the point where they are tasteless. Gravy is in a huge metal vat with a large layer of grease floating on top.

The pudding is actually quite nice, a huge chunk of chocolate sponge. But the custard is in a large vat, and it is lumpy; the lump falls apart to reveal powder. "I think it's Bird's Custard," says Jennie doubtfully, "but it's not like the Bird's we have at home." Similarly, the mashed potato is Cadbury's Smash, served from a huge vat and also full of powdery lumps. All of this is washed down with water from a plastic jug. I don't like drinking water anyway, but this has been enlivened by the previous shift adding salt and pepper to it. I have already given my dinner money in, and to be honest I don't think this is worth it.

The afternoon is a dizzying round of classrooms and teachers. We are issued with exercise books with the school crest on the front, and a book of plain paper known as a "rough book" for notes. We are issued with text books from a cupboard down in the basement. I arrived with a fountain pen in my brand new pencil case, but some of the girls think it is funny to push blotting paper into the inkwells.

At four o'clock, a bell rings. We pack up our satchels – I have put everything into my desk. We make our way down to the cloakroom, and change into our outdoor shoes and put on our macs. I don't have a blue felt school hat – Mom and Dad did find it expensive – so I tie on my navy blue head scarf, which is actually one of Mom's, over the offending ribbon. Then to one of the two front doors, past the porter's lodge, to where Mom is waiting outside the gate.

"How was it?" she asks anxiously. I am about to pour out the whole saga: the hair ribbon; how new and strange everything is; how ugly I think I look; how confused I am, rushing from room to room with my heavy satchel on my shoulder; the dreadful dinner. Then I look at her hands as she puts on her gloves, worn out with work, all to make money to send me here. "It was great," I say brightly. She smiles and takes my hand. We walk down Rose Hill Road to the 40E bus stop at the top of Villa Road.

3

Home and Away

1968–1970

And it gets better.

It seems to me that when we lived in Guildford Street, when we went on holiday, that the sun was always out, and that everything was lovely. The sun is still out, but things are maybe less lovely. Old Birmingham is disappearing under a tide of concrete. The Newtown Estate is ugly. My school uniform is ugly. I am uncomfortably aware of becoming a teenager. There are murmurings of industrial discontent. That Labour may go in the next election. That The Beatles are breaking up.

But on the whole, I am still enjoying myself. I'm now travelling on my own to school, a two bus journey. The bus is always full when it reaches my stop, so I have to sit upstairs in a cloud of cigarette smoke, rubbing a clear space onto the steamed up window as I read the *No Spitting* notices. This is still the old fashioned bus with a platform and conductor, and the driver sitting in a little compartment. The conductor has a little silver machine, and the tickets are all different colours. Often, she is a lady and they call her a clippie, and lots of them are Irish, as are the drivers. Birmingham City Transport had a recruitment office in Dublin in the 1950s, and lots of people came over to drive the buses or be a clippie. Dad has an Irish mate who drives the Outer Circle No 11 bus, and he told Dad it is "the best job in the world!"

The 40E is already one of the newer buses, with no clippie and one automatic door at the front. It's often running late, and I have to spring along

Rose Hill Road; being late means a visit to the Headmistress; three lates means a detention. I feel a thrill of pride as I make my way in the Girls' Entrance, past the Mr Wilcox's porter's lodge, to my classroom – 3Z is followed by Lower IVZ, then UIVZ, and I'm no longer bottom of the school.

At Christmas 1967, Nan gave me a Five Year Diary. It has a lock and key which is good, as Susie wants to read it. For five years, I record my activities on a daily basis, inspired possibly by the book we are reading at school, *The Diary of Anne Frank*. I have it by me now.

There is comfort in routine. Unpacking the contents of my satchel into my wooden desk. Filling my fountain pen at the inkwell. The register and Assembly in the lovely blue painted hall. Prayers and Notices. Hymns from *Songs of Praise* and readings from the King James Bible. The school team sporting results. The announcements of the meeting of the various societies: debating, drama, folk dance, choir, orchestra. The House meetings. The great school badge at the front of the Hall – *Dieu et Mon Droit*. The royal arms of England and Wales under the Tudors. Mondays are dinner money days. Mom, with a sigh, hands over their hard earned cash, and a week's bus fare, all in coppers and silver, and I stow it in my little blue purse.

We have all been handed little jobs to do: Flower Monitor, Ink Monitor, Door Monitor – she opens the door for the mistresses and we all spring up as they come in and go out. We have all been given a House to be in; at William Cowper I was in Yellow House, which was St David's – Red was St George, Blue St Andrew's and Green St Patrick's. Here, the houses are named after the royal dynasties of England – Normandy, Plantagenet, Lancaster, York, Tudor, Stuart, Hanover and Windsor. I am in Hanover, which seems dull, as Tudor would be more exciting because of the Six Wives of Henry the Eighth (I've just borrowed a book about them from Birchfield Library). We have termly House meetings under the house notice boards. We can get points for our house by taking part in school sports or winning something at the Flower Show.

English is still my favourite subject. The English teachers are younger than the other teachers, and they tend to have longer hair and shorter skirts. I like Mrs Davies, who tells me she is to be our form teacher in Upper IVZ. She gives us a reading list at the beginning of every term and I dutifully trot off to Birchfield Library to find the books, but they don't tend to be my favourites, Malcolm Saville, Elsie J. Oxenham, Ruby Ferguson, Lorna Hill and Elinor Brent-Dyer. I am being introduced to The Classics: I feel like a grown up.

Our texts are handed out at the beginning of the year, and all the books are kept in a small room next to the Playroom. It smells of ink and paper. We have a play, a novel and an anthology of poetry, and in the First Year they are *Great Expectations* and *A Midsummer Night's Dream*.

Miss Reid takes all the First Year for English; this is to get to know us. She takes lessons in her black gown, but the cap only comes out for Speech Day. She reads poetry to us, and we read poetry to her; this is accompanied by a patient correcting of our accents, which are those of Birmingham and the Black Country. My parents have hysterics when I come home saying "baath" instead of "baff". We recite "Everything, nothing, something", instead of the Brummie "Everythink, nothink, somethink". "Gs, ladies, not Ks!"

English is now split into Language and Literature. I compose a few poems and stories which are published in the school magazine, *The Beacon*. After English, I like French, which is taken by Mrs Wax, our form teacher. The only teaching aids in the 1960s are the chalkboard and chalk, so Mrs Wax chalks up the verbs on the board and we chant them, learning them off by heart – *Je suis, tu es, il est, elle est...*

Religious Studies, still known as Scripture, is another favourite taken by Mr Dolman, tall and thin and earnest. He tells us he is training to be a Methodist minister. The other Scripture teacher is Mr Arnold, who wants to be a missionary. Scripture is interesting because we do all the faiths and denominations of the world and then we write essays and have debates on complex subjects such as abortion.

Miss Hinton, soon to become Mrs Fletcher, is small and has long hair; she takes Geography. I like doing the countries of the world and chocolate and cocoa and tea, but I don't like the geology side. The Geography Room is full of interesting maps and globes.

Art is with Mr Tristram, who is middle-aged and enthusiastic (and one of the very few male teachers). The Art Room is another lovely room, full of exciting things like palettes and paint brushes, and it smells lovely. Even more exciting is a large potter's wheel for the benefit of the few girls doing Pottery O Level. Mr Tristram also offers calligraphy lessons for the benefit of girls whose handwriting is considered untidy, and sadly I am one of them.

Singing takes place in the Hall with Mr Billington. For some reason, we call him Archie, which is not of course his name. We are issued with song sheets Xeroxed in the school office, and trill *Nymphs and Shepherds*. None of us have very good voices, but if you are any good you are roped into singing with the School Choir. But even though I sang with William Cowper at the Town Hall in the Junior School's Concert, I am beginning to realise dimly that I am not any good at anything.

I love History with Mrs Thorne. She tells us she is writing a history of the school, but the history we do is from the Stone Age to the Atomic Age. We learn the names and dates of the Kings of England, the dates of the battles of the Wars of the Roses, the English Civil War, life in a medieval village, and the Anglo Saxon saints who brought Christianity to Britain (this is, after all, a church school).

For Music, we move down to the Music Room, which is down a set of steps next to the Play Room. Music is the same as at William Cowper – the recorder. The recorder is *cheap* and we are issued with the standard brown wooden school recorder, but I think I would like one of my own. Mom takes me off to Yardley's Music Shop at Snow Hill, and buys me a white wooden recorder for fourteen shillings and sixpence (be different), and Auntie Floss makes me a blue bag out of an old pillowcase to keep it in.

It is nice of Mom to do this, because I know they are short of money. Mom is still working evenings at Great King Street, but plans to go afternoons at Great Hampton Street when Susie starts at King Edward's as she undoubtedly will, as she is a whizz at Mathematics. So they need to save for that, as all their savings were spent on my uniform. And there is the rent. It was thirty shillings a week at Guildford Street, but now it is five pounds a week. The rent collector doesn't come round any more with his bag bulging with money; Dad pays it fortnightly by cheque, using his new bank account. And then there are the bills.

When we moved in, Dad was thrilled to find out that we had underfloor heating. It was June, but they switched it on to test it and then we have it on all over the cold winter of 1968/1969. The bill, when it comes in from Midlands Electricity Board, is *enormous*. They hastily switch it off, draw out their savings to pay the bill, and replace it by using the three bar gas fire in the living room, and a one bar electric fire in their room and in the kitchen. We are not allowed to have them in our room, and there is not one in the bathroom. Getting up in the morning, it is freezing, and we race to the bathroom and then downstairs to get dressed in front of the fire.

I have to be out of the house at eight o'clock, and it always seems to be winter, dark and raining. As it always seems to be when we take our weekly trips on the Corporation bus to the school playing fields. We run about on the hockey field in aertex blouses and skirts, green socks and hockey boots, and my lips and fingers turn blue with cold. Summer is better – athletics, rounders, long jump, high jump, and tennis at the new courts at the back of the school. I have my own tennis racket, and Mrs Craddock says I might get picked to play in the Fry Cup, which is the annual tennis tournament between the three girls' schools in the King Edward's Foundation.

Once a week we also head off on the Corporation bus for Swimming at Grove Street Baths, and practise for lifesaving badges. We all wear the school swimming costume, which is black with the school badge on, and costs 23/-.

The Gymnasium is a separate block at the rear of the school and in cold weather, we take a shortcut through the Boiler Room, where the janitor lives. For Gym, we have navy blue leotards and swing from ropes hung from the ceiling, or shin up ladders attached to the walls. I'm unable to leap over the vaulting horse, and I am uncomfortably unaware that unlike my heroines in the Chalet School, Malory Towers, or St Clare's, I am NOT good at games. But Games at least are enjoyable. There are subjects I really hate; Maths of course is first and foremost. It is taught by kind Miss Naish, but even she cannot make algebra, geometry, fractions and decimals comprehensible to me. As for the slide rule, it reduces me to actual tears, as do the logarithmic tables.

Science is enjoyable at first. We wear our navy blue or bottle green science overalls, and sit at benches in the Science Block. Miss Beechill lets us play with Bunsen burners, do experiments with chemicals, and make collections of matter in the school grounds. But as Science turns into physics, chemistry and biology, it is much harder and less fun.

Cookery is with Mrs Garrett, who is always beautifully dressed, coiffed and made up. Every week she gives us a list of ingredients for next week's cooking. Mom makes a face as she gets it, as it is not the type of food we eat – pineapple upside-down cake, Russian fish pie, gooseberry fool, are all swallowed by my dad with a groan. Making bread is more fun, but at home we just have Sunblest from the Co-op. Gutting fish is the worst week; after watching Mrs Garrett decapitate a fish, chop off its tail and gut its interior, some of us are close to fainting and secretly resolve to be off sick the week after. But the cookery room is nice, with its ovens around the wall, and we wear inevitably bottle green and navy blue cookery aprons, with our names embroidered on the front.

The embroidering is done in Needlework, on Friday afternoons with Miss Stock, tall and thin and dark of hair. We invent a romance for her with Mr Arnold of Scripture. At William Cowper we embroidered our names in cross stitch on little squares of cambric, but here we are soon introduced to the mysteries of the sewing machine, bias binding, tailors chalk, tacking pins and pinking shears. Once again, I have a huge list of stuff for poor Mom to purchase, and she has to go to Lewis's haberdashery department for this. We are making a dress and knowing I will never finish it, Mom buys me the cheapest material, checked pink and white cotton which will make me look like a tablecloth if I ever do finish it.

I have so many places to go for different subjects that Dad's friend Johnnie Bowman kindly makes me a printed timetable in a plastic cover, which I carry about like a talisman. The day is marked by the ringing of hand bells, as yet to be replaced with buzzers. Four o'clock is the best bell of all, even though as I pack my heavy satchel, I consult my homework diary and see I have two hours of homework. The Homework Monitors will collect our books in the morning, and stash them in a cupboard of labelled shelves right opposite the staff room.

Fountain pens with cartridges are beginning to replace pens needing to be filled, and the Ink Monitors can thankfully hang up their bottles of Quink; some of the girls are even beginning to write with a Biro. We are encouraged to cover our exercise books, for which most of us use wallpaper, though Mom does manage to get me some industrial plastic from work (with which I promptly cover my Armada paperbacks).

The school day, the school year, is marked by events and happenings which make it all just a bit more bearable. Morning and afternoon break bring milk and iced buns, or maybe a Penguin biscuit; we huddle round the radiators in the playroom (in which there is not actually anything to play with) and we talk about what we have seen on the telly, or what's in the *Jackie* magazine.

Dinner is not any better, but we can go after into the School Library. This is at the bottom of a corridor opposite the staffroom; the English Department staff are in charge of it and it has two rooms, one is lending and reference and the other is for the Sixth Form only. I spend happy lunchtimes browsing in the peaceful atmosphere.

There are societies you can attend at lunchtime – drama, flower arranging and debating. Girls join up simply to get out of the cold playroom, where the only activity is clinging to the radiator to keep warm. There are of course sporting activities, although I have just dimly realised that I am not good at sport. Some of the girls rush off at lunchtime for hockey or athletics down at the gymnasium, and it's just like all my books about boarding school, but it's no good for me.

The sporting activities are all leading up to Sports Day, which is once a term in the summer. We all traipse onto the Corporation buses lined up in Rose Hill Road and are transported to the playing fields for an afternoon of athletics. This is the summer term and we switch to the summer uniform, which is a navy blue or bottle green dress with thin black stripes, worn with a cardie and a straw boater. The boater is optional, but the dress is essential and as my parents spent all their savings on the new uniform, there is no money for the dress. My mother combs Birmingham and finds a very close copy in C&A, but as I sit on the grass at Sports Day with Jennie and Lesley, watching girls performing the high jump, the long jump, and running very fast, I am uncomfortably aware that I am different because we are much poorer.

The Summer Term also sees the Swimming Gala and the Fry Tennis Cup. The Swimming Gala sees us once more board the Corporation buses, this time to Woodcock Street Baths for an Inter House tournament. And I am in it, here is something I am good at, at last, I am swimming backstroke for Hanover House (mainly because I can't dive, only belly flop). I swim in my black KEGSH costume and rubber cap, but alas, I am last in my heat and Hanover House has no chance of winning the House Cup anyway. But Dad has been taking us to Kingstanding Baths since we were little, and I love the smell of the chlorine, the tiles, the stained glass, and the arched roofs of the old Victorian swimming baths.

I don't even attempt to put in an entry for the Flower Show, which also generates points for the House Cup, but it is lovely to look at all the displays in the playroom. Although we have now got flowers in our gardens, which Dad is turning into things of beauty. In fact, New John Street West has won the Birmingham's Best Kept Gardens award.

The Fry Cup Tennis Tournament is different. It is an inter schools tennis tournament between the six schools of the King Edward's Foundation, girls and boys (there is, of course, no such thing as mixed sports). We play Camp Hill and the High, and having played tennis since I was a little girl in the backyard, I am in the team for the final. Once more in our summer dresses, blazers and boaters, we board the Corporation buses for Edgbaston. I have my very own tennis racket in a cover; it was my last Christmas present from Lucas's Christmas party.

Once there, we have a wander around the school first, which is even more impressive than ours. Groups of the girls of the High keep stopping us and asking us if they can show us around; they have obviously been briefed. Their voices are so different from ours; this is South Birmingham, and a whole world away. My tennis match, like all the others, ends 6-0, 6-0, 6-0, playing in a backyard isn't the same as a grass court; and the buses crawl wearily back as the High triumphantly claims the Trophy yet again.

We don't have school trips anymore, as we did at William Cowper, to Dudley Zoo, Drayton Manor or Alton Towers. However, if there is a film showing somewhere that is relevant to what we are doing in History or English, we are taken off on the bus to see it, usually to the Gaumont or the Odeon Queensway (many of the cinemas of my childhood, such as the Orient, the Newtown Palace, or the Villa Cross, are now becoming Bingo Halls). We go off to see *Anne of the Thousand Days, Lawrence of Arabia, Far from the Madding Crowd* and *Dr Zhivago*. At this time, I want to be Julie Christie. Seventies Cinema is generally rather poor, though Mom and Dad enjoy James Bond and *The French Connection*.

The end of the school year sees a school production such as *Murder in the Cathedral, Noye's Fludd* or *The Italian Straw Hat*, and in a very futuristic way, these productions are what is now described as gender fluid, as we play all the male parts, often with our long hair knotted at our chins to form beards. The one exception is *Orpheus in the Underworld*, to our excitement a joint production with King Edward's Aston (boys!). There is also the annual publication of *The Beacon*, the school magazine, and at last, I get some House points, as some of my poems are printed in it. All the school awards, sports scores and examination results are printed in it, and are read out on Speech Day, when we return in September, a very grand affair with the Bailiff of the King Edward's Foundation and the Governors. The school choir sings, the orchestra plays, we trill the school anthem and we utter the Founder's Prayer with heartfelt enthusiasm as we are due a day off for Edward the Sixth's birthday. His portrait gazes down at us from the front of the hall, under the school coat of arms. And I have a prize for English – a book token, to be taken to the Midland Educational for a Monica Edwards, Noel Streatfeild or Malcolm Saville. Life is good.

It is a pity that my day concludes with a good two hours of homework, which leaves me little time to do anything very much. Our twelve inch black and white TV, which served us faithfully for so many years, looked so sad in our brand new living room that Mom and Dad pushed the boat out and bought a larger one on Hire Purchase from Rumbelows, still black and white, but with the addition of a channel we have never seen before – BBC Two. Susie and I have grown out of our childish programmes; our new enthusiasm is *Top of the Pops*, which Mom and Dad endure. There are a few programmes we all enjoy, such as *Daktari* and *Skippy the Bush Kangaroo*. As Mom doesn't get home till late from the night shift, we still have a diet of the Westerns and war films which Dad likes best, but they send us off to bed so they can watch

Come Dancing. And on Saturdays, we can still gather round the new telly together to watch *Dixon of Dock Green, The Morecambe and Wise Show, Val Doonican*, and as a special treat on Saturday night, *Match of the Day* (Dad still spends Saturday afternoons glued to *Grandstand*).

Mom is still using the little radio she had in Guildford Street, the aerial pulled to its full length, and she is faithful to the Light Programme (now Radio Two). But we have discovered Radio Caroline and Luxembourg; our Christmas presents in 1968 were transistor radios in brown leatherette cases with a shoulder strap, and we can listen to them at night under the bedclothes with the earplugs supplied.

The shops are closing down on Newtown Row and Lozells Road, and the buildings are being demolished. The old Spartan Steel factory is set to become a Royal Mail building. The Aston Hippodrome is now a bingo hall, the Orient Six Ways is closing, the Villa Cross is to become an Asian picture house. So if we want to go to the pictures, it has to be the Odeon New Street. There are even rumours that our old school, William Cowper, is to be demolished to make way for a new building. Old Birmingham is disappearing.

Dad is working hard on the gardens. They were derelict when we moved in, and he digs them over and puts in plants, flowers, trees and builds a crazy paving. We spend hours in the garden with Kim Harrison, playing Monopoly and Cluedo, when we aren't zooming over the estate on our bikes or roller skates. Susie is annoyingly good at Monopoly; within an hour, she has hotels on Mayfair, Park Lane and Bond Street, and I am bankrupt with one lonely house on the Old Kent Road.

Mom is now shopping at the Newtown Precinct, and actually we like it. We go with her on Saturday mornings, and the precinct is full of new shops. Only it's a shame that there isn't a Co-op, so we no longer quote our divvy number 173790. There are supermarkets, butchers, bakers, banks, furniture shops and a Newsagent's, Dillons, which delivers our papers now Cooper's has gone. Best of all is the Indoor Market, a round, concrete building full of dozens of stalls. We quickly discover a stall selling toys and it has a circular spinner of Armada paperbacks costing 2/6d, on which I can spend my birthday money.

Susie and I begin tap and ballet classes at the Hazeltree School of Dance, every Wednesday at the precinct. Mom gives us our sixpences. We are not very good at all, but live in hope. On Thursday nights, I go up to the youth club at the brand new St George's Church; this is built on a stretch of green in front of Lucas's Great King Street and people call it Lucas's Park, although it isn't.

Behind it is the brand new Newtown Health Centre, where Doctor Carolan now labours. It is a curious park – no swings, no slides, no flowers – all it has is a rather odd iron sculpture called Aeolus, The Wind God, which makes noises when the wind blows. I quite like it, but people locally call it the Ding Dong.

The youth club is run by the Reverend Geoffrey Brown. It's mainly ping pong and dancing to records in the basement of the church while the Reverend, who lives in a brand new house next to the church, circulates genially. I meet my old friend from William Cowper, Linda Broadfield, there. The Reverend is responsible for a lot on the estate: events at the church; the annual Newtown Bonanza, a huge event with parades; Miss Newtown and a jumble sale at the Settlement.

On Saturday afternoon, Mom now catches the 33 into town from Newtown Row instead of the Summer Lane 5 or 7, and we are allowed to go with her. We can wander around on our own while she goes down the Bull Ring for meat and fish. It doesn't take us long to find the records department in WH Smith, or the Midland Educational, or the wonders of Hudson's Bookshop. But best of all are the escalators in Lewis's and Rackham's and we spend happy hours riding up and down them. The lifts in Rackham's also have smart attendants in a snappy uniform, sitting on a flip down stool.

Sundays are usually days out in the car. Dad has replaced our faithful A40 with an A60, which he does not think much of. "British manufacturing is going to pot," he grumbles. "In twenty years, Germany and Japan will lead the world in car manufacturing and we'll be making cars for them." Our days out are our usual ones, the two parks at Perry Barr, Sutton Park, Aston Hall, the Clent Hills, the Lickey Hills and Cannon Hill Park. But sometimes our Sundays are spent over at the Atkins' house in Sutton Coldfield, Stan and Barbara are Mom and Dad's best friends; they grew up in Aston together and Dad and Stan worked at the BOC. Barbara now works as a cleaner at the Good Hope Hospital and their daughter Lynne is exactly my age; we grew up together. Their son Andrew is my Little Brother; he is always beautifully dressed in a shirt and shorts, and on Sunday a dicky bow, and our nickname for him, for no apparent reason, is Dicky Donut. A gentle soul, he joins in willingly with all our games. Their house at 27 Bedford Drive has the benefit of a back garden with a swing, so we love going there.

On Sunday nights, Mom and Dad go up to the Scott Arms in Great Barr and meet their friends: Pat and John Bowman, Harold and Clare Styles, Frank and Elsie Collins, Phil and Jim Grogan, John and Nora Nevin, Roy and Doreen McManus. We call them all Auntie and Uncle, and their children are our friends. Many of these people are Irish, and came over in the 1950s in search of work; they have all done very well. Great Aunt Floss usually comes round on Sunday afternoons for a cup of tea, but David and Mark, our childhood companions and cousins, no longer come with her.

Bank Holiday Mondays see an exodus of these people to somewhere like Stourport on Severn or Ross on Wye, where in the view of the children concerned, far too much time is spent with them sitting in the pub, while we hang about in the children's room, armed with a packet of crisps and a bottle of Vimto, and playing the one armed bandits in the children's rooms.

Our Easter holidays are still spent at Stan's caravan in Wales, but our summer holidays are now in a holiday camp in Cornwall with Mom and Dad's friends. Now that they are building the M5, the journey is much quicker despite the long tailbacks. We stay in something called a chalet, but some of the women are not happy about the shared bath and toilet facilities, which is odd because we all came from houses without them.

Our parents are obliging about taking us to the beach at Perranporth, and on days out to St Agnes, Mevagissey and Bodmin Moor, but what they like is to sit in the camp bar at night and watch a cabaret, consisting usually of a comedian or dancers. Lunch is cheese and tomato sandwiches on the beach, with a thermos of tea and an ice cream, and meals are usually fish and chips – international cuisine doesn't really exist yet. I just can't believe that people can grow up surrounded by such beauty, and we're always sad when it's time to come home.

Our first two Christmases at New John Street West are very different. It was just us at Guildford Street, as you couldn't ask people round to a house with no toilet or bathroom. Now Mom thinks she can. Christmas at school is not as good as at William Cowper; we begin to notice it is Christmas when we belt out the Advent hymns from *Songs of Praise: Hills of the North, rejoice! O come, O come, Emmanuel!* As Christmas comes closer, we are treated to Bible readings every morning on the Christmas story, and all the old favourite Christmas carols.

Of course, we no longer believe in Father Christmas and we don't go to the Christmas parties at Tucker Fasteners or Lucas's anymore. Christmas is still exciting though. Dad puts up the decorations and the tree at home, and School has a massive Christmas tree in the Hall as we sing the Advent and Christmas carols in Assembly. In Art, we design Christmas cards for the school. Susie and I pool our birthday money for presents for Mom, Dad and Nan, and I go off to the Midland Educational to buy presents for Jennie and

Lesley. Mom and Dad turn up for the school Carol Service, and we pick up our end of term reports. And there's end of term trips to the Station Street Repertory Theatre to see *The Rose and the Ring* and *1066 And All That*, which we are reading in English. I have never been to the theatre before, and I love the atmosphere, the music and the costumes (this lovely theatre is due to close and be replaced by a new building).

We now have the presents Mom and Dad think are more suitable for our ages – transistor radios in 1968, handbags in 1969. I also get a chemistry set complete with a Bunsen burner and lots of exciting smelling chemicals in test tubes. Our Christmas dresses are now from C&A Gear Cellar or Chelsea Girl, and Mom invites the rest of the family round for a buffet on Christmas night, accompanied by dancing to the year's records played on their new Hi Fi system which has replaced our faithful Dansette. And the telly is so good: *Disney Time, Ken Dodd, Christmas Night with the Stars, Morecambe and Wise.*

Mom and Dad always go out to a dinner dance on New Year's Eve with their friends, at somewhere like the King's West Bromwich, while we see in the New Year with Nan, and spend New Year's Day watching the sport with Dad, and Mom watches *The Newcomers.*

There is one more great event as the Sixties draw to a close. On the 20th July, 1969, Mom and Dad wake us very early, "You have to see this!" They almost carry us downstairs in the early dawn light and put us on the sofa. The curtains are still drawn. They turn the telly on and we blink; the telly is never on in the morning. And we see the grainy black and white pictures, on our grainy black and white telly, of the Moon landings. It seems a good omen for the decade ahead.

Yes, life was good between 1968 and 1970. But change is coming. The Seventies have arrived and with them death, divorce and illness for my family. And for Birmingham, industrial unrest, strikes and two bombs which will blow the heart out of our city. New beginnings are not always good. Omens are not always correct.

4

Hatches, Matches and Dispatches

1970–1971

Every night, Nan faithfully reads the Births, Marriages and Deaths in the *Evening Mail*. "I might see somebody I know," she says hopefully.

In the years we lived at Guildford Street, our family was complete. There was no illness, no deaths, no separations and we cousins played together as part of a large, extended family which lived close to each other and always met up at baptisms, weddings and funerals – the great working class family events. It is why the decade has a golden glow over it.

The Seventies strike with a chill wind, even though Dad welcomed in the new decade with a toast on New Year's Eve. Our dog, Skipper, who came with us from Guildford Street, disappears when out walking with my sister. He simply runs off, and we never see him again, though we search fruitlessly for him. It is a loss my sister and I feel to this day.

Dad takes us up to the Birmingham Dogs' home in Digbeth. I don't like to see all the dogs looking for a home, but we end up with a little black mongrel, Sarah, who will be our beloved companion for the next twenty years. She is called after Mrs Bricknell's spaniel, at Bigbury Farm; the Bricknells are now retired and living in a bungalow in Totnes; we always call in to see them en route to Cornwall. It's a good thing we have a dog of our own because our childhood companion, Laddie the collie, Uncle Bill's dog, is run over and killed in Sutton Coldfield at the beginning of 1970. Another loss. "Lassie, off the telly," the children at William Cowper used to call out, when Mom walked him to school when she fetched us.

Then my uncle Charlie dies. He was Dad's eldest brother and he was only in his late forties. Uncle Charlie was married to our Auntie Lil, a widow who has two daughters, Eileen and Maureen, and she is the mother of our cousin John, tall with dark curly hair. Mom and Dad go off to the funeral, Mom all in black, and Dad wearing a black arm band. "It was his war wounds," he says, subdued. "He never recovered – he was bent over double."

Another family tragedy strikes at the Holtes. My Auntie Jean, Dad's sister, and Uncle Ray have a little girl, our cousin Zara. Zara, a pretty little blonde who wears lovely frocks at family events, was born with kidney disease and dies aged only nine. At the funeral, Mom cannot stop herself from weeping when she sees the small coffin. Jean and Ray still have a son, Paul, but he is diabetic and frail and dies at the age of eighteen, when Jean and Ray both try and commit suicide (a family tragedy still in the future).

Marriages begin to break up. There are rumours that Aunty Eileen's husband is seeing another woman. Eventually, he leaves her and she drifts away with our cousins Dean and Tracey. It is the same with Uncle Charles and Auntie Ann, and after their break up, we do not see our pretty cousin Marie with her swept up blonde hair for many years.

Worst of all, the marriage of our Uncle John and Auntie June breaks up. Our pretty Auntie June, the epitome of Sixties glamour, who looks "just like Dusty Springfield," as my dad remarks approvingly, disappears from our life forever. Susie, who was her beloved niece, is truly upset. "I didn't know people could go, just like that," she says, subdued. This is of course before the days of the Internet and social media, and nobody in our family has a phone even though Dad talks of getting one.

There is one bright spot in this sadness. Uncle John moves in temporarily with Nan, sleeping on her sofa. He comes over to see Mom and Dad, smoking at the dinner table, and every Saturday morning he calls in dressed in his cricket whites, on his way to a game. Over six feet tall, with black hair and brown eyes, he looks wonderful; Mom and Nan have washed all week to get those whites immaculate. We still only have the twin tub, but there is a launderette in the precinct. Even better, he calls round to take us swimming in the brand new Newtown Baths, in the precinct.

Despite family sadness, we think we have something to look forward to in 1970. Susie is sitting her eleven plus, and will hopefully be joining me at King Edward's and it is my first teenage birthday in February. We love Uncle John's visits and visits by Floss, Uncle Bill and Auntie Margaret from Sutton Coldfield. My dad's brother, Uncle Albert, comes over from Wolverhampton with my Auntie Mary and my cousins Jim and Janet. Janet is already a teenager and I admire her clothes. Although now crippled by arthritis, Auntie Mary has a wonderful Black Country sense of humour.

We enjoy also swimming, trips to Birchfield Library, and the school of dance. Then Dad decides, in order to cheer us up, that we can at last have our own bedrooms. Susie doesn't want this ("Look after your little sister") so in order to console her, she is allowed to have the front bedroom, which is the larger, and looks out on the front garden, where Dad has laid a lawn and a flowerbed.

So I am in the small room at the back, but I don't mind. I can look out from the window on the back garden, where Dad is building a crazy paving, all different colours. The bottom of the garden is lawn with a flowerbed, and best of all, Dad has planted a laburnum tree which will grow up to my window. The back garden is also the home of the shed, which is Dad's kingdom, and home to his gardening tools.

There is no money for my room; it is beige or rather magnolia, as all the house is ("I'll get round to wallpapering next year!"). Dad moves in my bed, a small wardrobe, and best of all my little white bookcase with all my Chalet School and pony and ballet paperbacks. I have the table from the living room at Guildford Street, and Mom hangs a piece of curtain net over it, and puts on my hairbrush and comb and a stand up mirror. This is my dressing table. She also buys some pink and white curtains from the market at the Newtown precinct, and I think my very own bedroom is lovely.

We hope that things cannot get worse, from now things can only get better. It is, after all, the start of a new decade. Which will surely be a good one for the family, Birmingham and Britain. January 1970 is a snowy month, the days are short. I struggle on my four bus journey through the snow – King Edward's never closes. Lesley, Jennie and I cling to the radiators in the playroom at dinner time. At night, after doing my homework, I enjoy some of the telly programmes I am interested in now – *The High Chaparral* and *The Six Wives of Henry VIII* (soon followed by Glenda Jackson in *Elizabeth R*), *The Virginian* and for light relief *Oh, Brother!* and *On the Buses* on our much bigger but still black and white telly. We can't find anything to watch on BBC Two, but Dad does do the Open University on it.

Sunday January 25th is a day like any other. Nan comes over and Dad goes to fetch Floss. Dinner is Sunday roast and blackberry crumble with custard. After, Mom sits at our dining room table and chats to Floss, Dad washes up and Nan stands next to him, drying. Susie and I are on the floor, playing with the new puppy. A sudden thump makes us all stand up and turn round. Standing next to Dad, Nan has fallen backwards and falls to the floor, still clutching her tea towel. She falls straight, like a tree being felled. The thump was her head hitting the floor (many years later, I hear somebody on a TV detective programme remark that a body always crumples as it falls. This is not true. She fell straight and lay on the floor like that).

Pandemonium reigns. Mom and Floss scream, the dog barks, Susie and I jump up. Dad scoops her up – she is as light as a feather – and carries her into the living room, where he lays her on the sofa. Then he runs up to the call box to call 999. Floss is tending to Mom, who is having hysterics, Susie and I look at Nan's face – so white, eyes closed, her mouth open. The ambulance comes very quickly and Mom and Dad follow it in the car. Floss puts us to bed. We hear them get back later and Dad takes Floss home, to save her getting the circle bus. I fall asleep weeping.

I wake up very early the next morning. I hear Dad get up. It is pitch black, but he is used to it, as he has to be at work for seven-thirty. I hear him get washed and dressed in the cold, dark house, then the door slams as he goes out. I wait. He is back fifteen minutes later; he has been to the call box. I hear him go into Mom's bedroom and he closes the door. There is silence.

He comes out after ten minutes. He goes into Susie's room. Then my door opens at last, he has Susie with him, blinking in her nightdress. He puts her into bed with me, then he begins to speak. "You know your Nan was ill last night...." But I interrupt him, "She's dead!"

Nan was 61. She had been receiving her old age pension for only four months, which helped her cut down on the hard manual cleaning she had been doing since the war. Dad tells us it was a stroke or a blood clot on her brain. Then he says we are not going to school today, he will go and phone our schools and tell them.

He spends a long time at the call box and luckily this is in the days before they were vandalized; he has to phone every single member of the family, or get messages to them. Susie and I sit side by side for a bit in frozen silence. We are too young to be able to comfort each other and we are listening to the sound of sobbing coming from Mom's room. We have never seen our mother cry.

The rest of the day is dreadful. It is dark and cold and the curtains are drawn. We get ourselves up and go downstairs. Mom, in her dressing gown, is propped up in an armchair, covered with a blanket; she gives us a dead stare and continues crying. Members of the family arrive, all in deep states of shock. Somebody makes us lunch, and Auntie Margaret cooks us dinner. Very little notice is taken of us; they are too busy fussing over Mom. "I realise now," says Auntie Margaret many years later, "that we should all have spent more time with you two. I regret that now."

By nine o'clock, everybody has gone. Dad tells us he will be at home for a few days. There are things he has to do, he says, register the death and arrange the funeral. We will have to go back to school on Tuesday, because we will be looked after there. We are quietly sitting in the living room, at Mom's feet, polishing our school shoes. Dad sits on the arm of her chair, his arm around her. "They've been so good," he says, nodding at us. She looks at us. Her face is dead, no emotion at all. It seems as if she hates us. Then, to our horror, she begins to cry again. We flee upstairs, to our separate bedrooms, which are no longer a consolation.

On the following dark morning, we get ourselves up and washed and dressed. Susie has to walk off alone to William Cowper, down the safe Attenborough Close, next to the flats and away from the main road, but she looks very small and forlorn. Rather dreadfully, on Wednesday she is sitting her much anticipated eleven plus. She asks timidly if this will still go ahead. "Your Nan would have wanted it," says Dad gently.

He drives me to school, not thinking I am up to a four bus journey. He will pick me up at four o'clock, he says. He gives me my dinner money and a letter for Mrs Wax, my form teacher, explaining my absence. I know what it says. I go into Lower IVZ, Room 27, to exclamations from the other girls, but I go straight to the desk where Mrs Wax is sitting with the Register and hand her the letter. I can't bear to watch her while she reads it. "This is from Dad," I say. "It's to say why I wasn't in school yesterday. You see, my nan died." She looks taken aback, but reads the letter. Then she stands up and puts her hand on my shoulder. "I'm very sorry," she says gently. "I should go through the day as normal, it might help, but if you do feel bad at any point, ask if you can go and sit quietly in the library, or go to the sick room."

Word spreads quickly among the mistresses and girls. Nobody says anything, but everyone is very kind. Jennie and Lesley walk around with me at playtime. The first lesson is English and Mrs Davies lets me read Hermia in *A Midsummer Night's Dream*, because she is small like me. In French with Mrs Adie, we are doing La Famille, and we are drawing pictures of our family. I look at the one I have drawn of my nan, saying she is soixante-et-un. I raise my hand. Mrs Adie comes over.

"What is the French for dead?" I ask.

"Mort or morte," she says puzzled.

"Merci." I carefully rub out what I have already written and add *Ma grandmère est morte*. I am careful to add the feminine ending to *mort*. She is now opposite my *grandpère*, who is already *mort*.

"All my grandparents now *sont morts*," I say brightly. Mrs Adie shakes her head. She also touches my shoulder, and quickly moves on.

This is 1970. There is no bereavement counselling, no emotional health counselling. They are doing what they can. Dad is there to meet me at four o'clock. He takes me home and we have tea in silence.

The rest of the week is awful. Dad is off work all week, arranging the funeral. I know this means he won't get paid and he is worrying about money, because Mom, who only moves from her bed to her armchair, is also off work and not earning. Dr Carolan makes a rare home visit to see her; he shakes his head as he tells Dad he knows nothing of bereavement and depression, but he will prescribe tranquilisers. This has a rather zombie-like effect on her. Members of the family drift in and out. Both Floss and Auntie Margaret come up trumps, turning up at the weekend to cook all the meals. We overhear them on Sunday, talking to Mom. "You've got to pull yourself together, Lily, for the sake of Bill and the girls."

But she doesn't.

With Uncles John and Bill, Dad goes over to Nan's flat. It has to be emptied as soon as possible and the keys returned to the Council, as nobody can afford to pay the rent. Her last budgie, the blue and white Joey, goes to her neighbour, Mrs Green. Everything else is packed up and boxed up for the Salvation Army to collect, because she always liked standing outside Rackham's at Christmas, listening to them play. Nan had nothing of value. She had no bank account and all the money she left is in her purse; her cleaning wages and her old age pension. She was a war widow and a poor cleaner, but her clothes and hats are immaculate, which makes me gulp as they are packed into boxes.

Members of the family take souvenirs. Her jewellery is costume jewellery and paste, strings of pearl beads and marcasite brooches. Dad takes her wedding ring for Mom, but he gives me her engagement ring from 1930, gold with a couple of small diamonds. "Because you were the eldest," he says. I have it still.

Her funeral takes place the week after at Witton Cemetery, in deep snow. She is interred with her first husband, but none of the grandchildren go, because the sight of my mom's grief is held to be too awful for us. Dad has keys to New John Street West made for us, as obviously we cannot any longer go round to Nan's when they are not at home. We are now latchkey children.

After Nan's funeral, the family begins to drift apart. She held it together, though Floss and Bill and Margaret are still faithful visitors.

1970 is a dreadful year. Mom does not go back to work, and we are very short of money. She sits in her armchair all day and cries. The curtains are always drawn in the house, so it is always dark. Dad has to be Mom and Dad to us.

Susie passes her Eleven Plus, but there is no outpouring of joy as there was when I passed. It is Dad who takes her, very subdued, to the new intake evening and goes with her to Horne Brothers to get her school uniform. They are so short of money that she has to wear my cast offs.

My birthday on the 5th February, when I become a teenager, passes without comment.

If there are any school trips to the cinema, I don't tell Dad because I know he hasn't got the seven and sixpence for them. I change my bus route; I start getting off the No 70 at Lucas's Great Hampton Street, and walking through the estate. This saves the bus fare into Birmingham and out and I can tell Dad I've still got money in my school purse for bus fare. I also tell him I want to take sandwiches into school instead of school dinner (which is no great loss), to save him school dinner money.

The girls and mistresses at school are kind and Kim Harrison is a faithful visitor, encouraging us to come and ride our bikes across the estate, or to roller skate, or to cut *Bunty* dress up dolls out of paper or to play Pirates on the bomb peck opposite the house, where we build a ship out of old planks. And Floss and Auntie Margaret still come round and cook for us. But this doesn't compensate for having a mother who is clearly having a nervous breakdown and looks at us as though she hates us.

And for me, it all comes to a head.

It is a Friday afternoon in the Spring Term. I hate Fridays because it is triple Needlework with Miss Stock and I have had huge problems with my sewing machine. At the four o'clock bell, I hurry out of school, lugging my heavy satchel, and fall headlong down the flight of steps at the front. My knee is grazed and bleeding, my sock is torn, but worst of all, I have scuffed my school shoes, and I know Dad can't afford another pair. I wait at the 40E bus stop at the top of Villa Road; there is a very large bee buzzing around. Normally, I wouldn't mind this – it is a sign of spring – but it won't leave me alone and I'm frightened of being stung. I'm on my own, because none of the other girls live this way; they all catch the bus in the other direction.

The 40E is late; it has a very circular route. I hurry through the underpass at Six Ways, my shoulder hurting from my satchel strap. I stumble again and all the contents of my satchel fall out; they are blown about in the breeze and I have to run all over the underpass, which smells, to pick them all up. At last, I am at the bus stop, waiting for a 33, 51, 52 or 59 to take me down Newtown Row. I think of arriving home in a dark house with the curtains drawn and a weeping mother, of the long, desolate weekend that lies ahead. My shoulder hurts where my now untidy satchel strap rests on it, my socks are torn and dirty, my knee is bleeding and my shoes are scuffed.

I start to cry.

This is the first time I have cried since Nan died. There are very few pedestrians on this stretch of the A34, by the Six Ways underpass, so I can cry as much as I want, and I cry till my eyes are red and my face is swollen, standing leaning on a wall at the bus stop. Then I see a 33 coming. It is one of the old fashioned buses which are disappearing now with an open platform, a driver's cubicle, and a conductor with a silver ticket machine. Despite the state of my face, which I hastily rub with my cotton hankie, I flag it down because I like these buses better than the newer ones, with the automatic doors opening at the front, and a driver who takes the fare at the wheel.

It stops and I get on. The conductor is standing on the platform; he is Jamaican, perhaps in his 30s. He looks very smart in his navy blue uniform, with his silver ticket machine slung around his neck. There were some families on Guildford Street who came over on the *Windrush*, and a lot of the men work for Birmingham City Transport, and their wives work cleaning the hospitals. Dad said they were essential workers, doing the work, the hours that nobody else wanted to do.

He takes a quick look at me. "You all right, now?" he asks. His voice is soft and lilting, so different from the voices of Birmingham and the Black Country. I mumble something about dust in my eyes. He is not convinced. He looks around. "You sit there now," he orders, pointing at one of the two sideways facing seats next to the platform. Reluctantly, I sit down; I had been hoping to slink upstairs. But he wants me where he can see me. He walks up and down, taking fares, but he doesn't take one from me. He does produce a crumpled but clean Kleenex, though. Every time he passes, he says, "Eyes all right, now?" He watches me the whole length of the journey.

The bus bumps over Six Ways, down Newtown Row, past the now closed Orient Cinema and the Bartons Arms, past Spartan Steel and William Cowper. I shoulder my satchel and get up as soon as the stop before the Newtown Palace, once a cinema now a bingo hall, where I get off, but he sounds the bell for me. He pronounces, "Eyes all right now!" "Yes," I say as I climb down from the platform. I stand at the bus stop and he rings the bell. The bus moves off, and he is still standing and looking at me. He raises his hand and shouts, "You take care of yourself, now!" It is like a blessing. I wave back.

I would like to say after this incident, that things got immediately better, but of course, they didn't. But what did happen was that I became aware of the kindness of strangers. He was himself a stranger in a strange land and he cared about a sad little girl. This was fifty years ago and I remember it as if it were yesterday. And I never said thank you then, so I'm saying it now. Thank you.

The year inevitably drags itself to a close. Dr Carolan makes regular visits to my mother. In September, she announces she will go back to work soon, but she will never return to the evening shift at Great King Street, she will go up to Great Hampton Street and ask for an afternoon job. She is also giving up being a shop steward. Something has died in her.

Before this happens, Susie begins King Edward's in September. I feel very sorry for her, as Mom has shown no interest in this. She will not go up to the school with her, and Dad cannot take any more time off work. We are very stretched financially. "You're in charge of her," Dad says resignedly. Susie looks very small and lost in her uniform when we set out. It is far too big. She has her dinner money and her bus fare in her regulation navy blue school purse, and her hair tied back neatly in a ponytail with a navy blue ribbon.

By now, I have worked out several bus routes, and I have decided to show all of them to her. We start with the one I started with, the No 5 or 7 down Summer Lane, get off at the bottom, cross over and catch one of the 70 buses to Soho Road, outside Yardley's Music Shop and the YMCA. There are several buses that can be caught from this stop. I peer anxiously up to Snow Hill (I am too vain to wear my glasses outside), and I swing around. "The No 70 is coming!" I stop. Susie is leaning against the bus stop. There are tears in her eyes, she slithers slowly down it, till she is on the pavement. New school, new uniform, everything strange, grandmother dead, mother having a nervous breakdown. This is her meltdown moment and I am not equipped to deal with it. I manage to get her up, onto the bus, and sit next to her. I get her to school, I deliver her to her new form and form teacher.

I think about her all day. But when I go and fetch her at four o'clock, she is chatting happily to her new form mates. We go down to the cloakroom, change our shoes, put on our navy blue macs. I tie on her headscarf. "I think I like it here," she says as we set off for the 40E bus stop. We have both learned that life, indeed, does go on.

5

New Beginnings

1970–1973

Of course, I have visions of taking over the running of the household and being a mother to Susie, rather like Katy in *What Katy Did*. This does not, of course, happen. Dad is running the house and Floss and Margaret are coming over at the weekend to cook. Susie doesn't want another mother. She is spending more and more time with Kim Harrison, as the age gap between us finally begins to show. And I am spending more time on school pursuits. There is no such thing as emotional health counselling in the 1970s, but there are other things that help. Carrying on as usual. It is peaceful at school, sitting in our rows of desks, bent over our books, dressed identically, in the pursuit of knowledge. The smell of ink. The blackboard and chalk. The scent of flowers drifting in through the windows in summer. Walking the playground with Lesley and Jennie. A timetable that is the same from every day to every week. The comfort of routine. The calm, unflappable teachers.

The events never change: The Flower Show, Sports Day, Founder's Day, the Christmas Carol concert, the Swimming Gala, the Fry Cup, the annual play, the Spring Fair jumble sale and Speech Day. Even the twice yearly exams. I never sat an exam before the Eleven Plus, and now I am doing them at Christmas and in the summer term.

We are very short of money without Mom's wages and Dad is struggling to pay the rent. Susie and I are practising small economies: taking sandwiches instead of school dinners, getting off the bus early and walking through the estate to save bus fare, keeping quiet about school trips. I want piano and violin lessons, but I daren't ask, as there is no money. Saddest of all, our roll of comics from Dillon's in the precinct is cancelled, Dad does replace it with the teenage comic *Jackie,* and we anxiously scan the Cathy and Claire problem page, but nobody is having problems like us. It is all spots and periods and the boy you saw at the bus stop who you fancy.

It comes to a head when Susie has to have my school pullover. There is no money to buy me another. It is OK to wear a navy blue cardigan, so Floss knits me one. It is a beautiful cardigan, she is a wonderful knitter, but it is not quite navy blue and it is not a school cardigan. I stand out and Miss Reid comments on it. I creep about, trying not to be seen. Susie is uncomfortably aware of wearing my cast offs, which are too big.

Then there is the problem of our shoes. Dad cannot afford the standard school shoes – we need two pairs, inside and outside, to be carried in our turkey red shoe bags, hung up in the cloakroom – so we have to have cheap copies from the shoe shops in the precinct. Visits to Clarks on the Lozells Road where they measured our feet are a thing of the past. And either because of the hardness of the school corridors, the fact that we are moving about all day, the walks around the playground, the cheapness of the shoes, or all of these, our heels don't last. There is no question of new shoes, so Dad takes them over and over to the cobbler, till one day he comes in triumphantly with my brown shoes. The cobbler has added steel tips to the sole and toes.

I am already embarrassed enough about these shoes, they are brown, rather than black, and as the mistresses have commented mildly, the heel is too high. I blurt out that they were in a sale, they were cheap, and they exchange knowing looks and say no more. And to add insult to injury, I am tapping around the school like Ginger Rogers; I can be heard coming miles off.

At this point, Mom realises she has to go back to work. There is an event that triggers her interest: the Equal Pay for Women Act, agreed on the 29th May 1970. This is something that she, as a shop steward, has always been interested in, especially since the Ford machinists' strike in 1968. "At last," she says to me, "I'll be paid the same as the men for doing the same job that the men do."

She doesn't go back to evenings on Great King Street, though. She goes up to Great Hampton Street and gets a job as a fitter in the afternoons. She is no longer a shop steward, and doesn't want to arrange the social events or be an Auntie at the Christmas parties any more. She is different. And Susie and I are indeed latchkey children, catching the bus home at four o'clock, getting off outside Lucas's so we can cast a wistful eye up at her window, and walking through the estate in time to catch a bit of afternoon TV, *Jackanory, Blue Peter,* or *Captain Scarlet and the Mysterons.* These seem a bit childish for us now and we are interested in programmes like *Doomwatch* and *The Champions* (Alexandra Bastedo is added to my Dad's "Isn't she beautiful?" list). And on Saturday, there are *The Banana Splits* and *Wacky Races.*

There are changes for Dad, too. His hero Harold Wilson lost the General Election on 18th June, and there is a Conservative Government under Edward Heath in place. Dad promptly leaves the Labour Party, or rather doesn't renew his subscription. "Well, at least he'll take us into the Common Market," he remarks, "but the Unions will soon bring him down." And indeed, Mom and Dad do vote to join what is known as the European Communities in 1973. "Because they support paid maternity leave," says my mom with a flicker of her old fire; she lost her job twice when she became pregnant.

Dad is sorry that Jennie Lee loses her Cannock seat. It was Jennie Lee who brought in the Open University, as her husband Aneurin Bevan brought in the NHS. Dad is now studying with the OU, as he intends to be promoted to foreman, and then manager. Instead of getting up to listen to the OU on the Home Service, he can now watch it on BBC Two, which we get for the first time. Huge packs arrive in the post. He is also going to evening classes at Birchfield Technical College, to do Public Speaking, as is his mate, Johnnie Murray. Johnnie, a softly spoken Irishman, now lives in Perry Barr with his wife Maureen and children Ann-Marie and Paul. He is chargehand, aiming to become foreman when Dad goes for Toolroom Supervisor. "It's so people don't laugh at our accent and think we're thick," explains Dad. "They always think the Irish and Brummies are thick." This puzzles me very much. I love Dad's and Johnnie's voices, and despite having left school at 14, they are very clever and very well read. All their friends are doing well too – Johnnie Bowman, also from Ireland, is now regional manager at the BOC.

Another event cheers Mom up greatly. Uncle John gets married again. He met Auntie Carol in a nightclub in Birmingham; she is from Bearwood and works in a library. She brings me books for my Latin project on Roman villas in Britain. She is very lovely, with curly brown hair and large dark eyes. They marry at the Registry Office, and we all pose for photos in the shadow of the statue of the Golden Boys, Boulton, Watt and Murdoch, me in my new pink coat from C&A. They buy a house on Mansfield Road in Aston, which is handy for Uncle John to help Dad with his Friday night pools round. We are still short of money, but the pools round means fish and chips from the chippie known as the Greek's on a Friday night.

Auntie Carol produces a new cousin for us, Jason, named after Uncle John's favourite TV show, *The Adventures of Jason King*, with debonair Peter Wyngarde. And after ten years of marriage, my Auntie Margaret has two sons in succession, my cousins Mark and Matthew. Susie and I are almost old enough to be their very young mothers, but it makes up a bit for losing Dean, Tracey and Marie.

My mother also has some surprising news. "Your Auntie Barbara is expecting... at the age of forty!" She rolls up her eyes. There are rumours of something known as The Pill, but this is rare with working class women. Auntie Barbara produces a little blonde girl to be christened Joanne Coral, after huge deliberations on Auntie Barbara's part. At the christening, we hear the vicar say, "I much prefer Coral, you know." For some reason, Susie and I think the vicar is wearing glossy pink lipstick, which makes us giggle. When he lowers Joanne into the font, he looks ups, grins, and announces, "I name this child Coral Joanne!" At which of course Susie, Lynne, Andrew and I burst into fits of giggles under glares from Mom and Auntie Barbara. But we do enjoy taking Jo for walks in her pushchair.

There are changes at school too. We are coming up to the O Level years and whereas before, we all did the same subjects, we now have to pick from a series of columns what we are going to do. This is leading up to our O Levels in 1973, and all that is fixed is that we all have to do English and Maths. I would rather not have to do Maths. Kind Miss Naish explains what she can about slide rules, logarithms and decimals, but it is like another language to me. Worse than another language. I love French with Mrs Adie, so that is a given, as rather oddly is Latin with the excellent Miss Boggis, deputy head and classicist. In fact, I would have preferred to do German with the genial Herr Mayer. Dad is the only person I can consult on my choices; it would be hopeless with Mom. He thinks it over.

"No, Herr Mayer is German. You know how your mom is about the war, and how she is now..." He stops. Yes, we all know how she is now.

"I just can't see her with Herr Mayer on Parents' Evening."

"Herr Mayer is Austrian," I say.

"Well, Hitler was Austrian."

I'm sorry to drop Geography with Mrs Fletcher, a tiny genial lady with long hair, but I'm doing Scripture instead with Mr Dolman, a tall thin man who is training to become a Methodist minister. Mr Arnold has left to be a missionary. History with Mrs Thorne is also a given. The things that I rather enjoy are all gone: Art, Pottery and Cookery. But I'm not sorry to say goodbye to Needlework.

We're all a bit cross that we stop swimming, but that PE and Games are still compulsory, as none of us are die hard sports fans. In fact, the main sport under discussion in school is football. I seem to be the only Villain amongst a crowd of Baggies. Boing Boing. UTV.

My big mistake is Science. I am not good at Science and I should put down the option of General Science, but I am seduced by the sound of Physics, Chemistry and Biology, the bottle green or navy blue overalls, the experiments with test tubes and Bunsen Burners, the Science Block with its rows of desks and surfaces and sinks. It's Madame Curie's fault.

And so the slip of paper with my O Level choices is submitted for better, for worse. I'm not thinking too much about the O Levels. I have other things to worry about.

Mom and Dad with cousin Jason at his christening, 1972.

Kim Harrison, myself and Susie with Sarah the dog.

A 70s Christmas with Lynne and Andrew Atkins.

Mom and Dad and friends enjoying life in the 1970s.

Me in the garden at New John Street West with Sarah the Dog, and Thornton House behind me, 1972.

Mom and Dad in the 1970s – note Dad's kipper tie!

Our smaller 1970s family – Uncle John, Auntie Carol, Auntie Margaret, Auntie Floss and Uncle Bill.

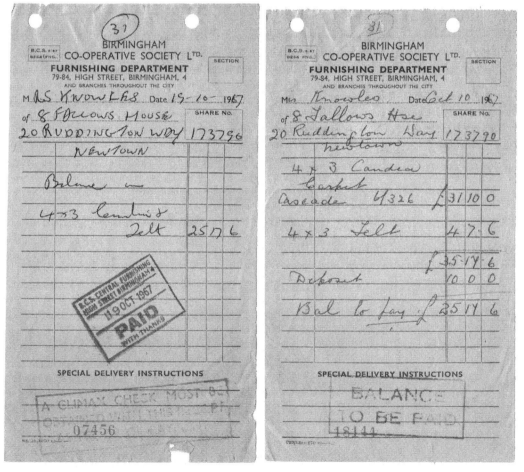

CITY OF BIRMINGHAM HOUSING MANAGEMENT DEPT.

TENANTS' DEPOSITS

Nº 13078   10th October 196_7_

Received from Mrs E Knowles

the sum of THIRTY SHILLINGS, being Deposit in respect of House

No. 8 Fallows Hse Newtown 19

For the Housing Management Committee,

Cashier

1   10   -

Nan's deposit for the keys of 8 Fallows House.

BIRMINGHAM
CO-OPERATIVE SOCIETY LTD.
FURNISHING DEPARTMENT
79-84, HIGH STREET, BIRMINGHAM, 4
AND BRANCHES THROUGHOUT THE CITY

MRS KNOWLES Date 19-10-1967
of 8 FALLOWS HOUSE   SHARE No.
20 RUDDINGTON WAY   173796
NEWTOWN

Balance

4x3 Carpet &
Felt   25 7 6

B.C.S. CENTRAL FURNISHING
HIGH STREET BIRMINGHAM 4
19 OCT 1967
PAID
WITH THANKS

SPECIAL DELIVERY INSTRUCTIONS

07456

BIRMINGHAM
CO-OPERATIVE SOCIETY LTD.
FURNISHING DEPARTMENT
79-84, HIGH STREET, BIRMINGHAM, 4
AND BRANCHES THROUGHOUT THE CITY

Mrs Knowles Date Oct 10 1967
of 8 Fallows Hse   SHARE No.
20 Ruddington Way   173790
newtown

4 x 3 Carpet
Cascade   4326   £31 10 0
4 x 3 Felt   4 7 6
                       £35 17 6
Deposit   10 0 0
Bal to pay £25 17 6

SPECIAL DELIVERY INSTRUCTIONS

BALANCE
TO BE PAID
18144

Nan's receipt from the Co-op for some new furniture and carpet for 8 Fallows House.

Dad and Susie with the much hated Austin A60 Cambridge.

KEGSH School purse, tie and badge. By kind permission of the members of the KEGSH Facebook page.

KEGSH Prefect badge. By kind permission of the members of the KEGSH Facebook page.

Miss Reid.

Miss Sargeant.

Miss Boggis, Deputy Head, on her 100th birthday, with Mrs Adie (French). Courtesy Alix Dearing.

KEGSH in 1968, when I began school there, copyright University of Birmingham Institutional Research Archive (the Phyllis Nicklin collection).

Birmingham Central Library exterior under construction.

Central Library interior under construction.
All photos on this page courtesy Birmingham
Archives Service.

Harold Wilson at the opening of the new
Central Library in 1974.

Newtown Community Centre.

St George's Church, Newtown.

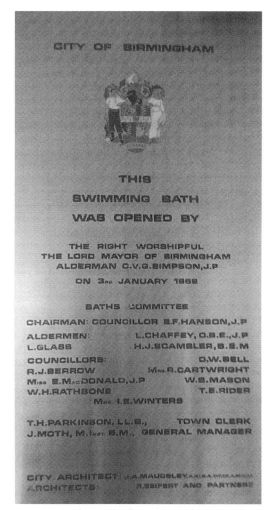

The early days of the Newtown Estate.

Swimming pool plaque. All photos on this page courtesy of Newtown Memories Facebook page.

Newtown swimming pool interior.

The Newtown News *is delivered to our house by Miss Newtown, 1968.*

Photo of me by the Rev Geoffrey Brown, accompanying an article called Off to University in the Newtown News, September 1975.

Littlewood's, 1969, copyright Barbara Smith.

6

The Trials, Tribulations, Troubles and Traumas of being a Teenager – and Occasional Triumphs

1970–1973

I become a teenager in 1970 and Susie in 1971 at which time our lives, and our Mom, are about as returned to normal as they are ever going to be. In fact, our parents take no notice of these monumental dates. "We were never teenagers," says Mom. "One day we were children on the school bench, and the next day a fourteen year old on the factory bench, making munitions as they dropped bombs on Birmingham. This teenage stuff, it all comes from America – James Dean, Sandra Dee, the bobby-soxers – all that sort of stuff. Not that they didn't seem to be enjoying themselves."

Well, she has a point.

Our first indication of being teenagers was the cancellation of our beloved comics from Cooper's Newsagent's and their replacement with a teenage magazine called *Jackie*. Apart from our fascination with the Cathy and Claire page (I see a boy at the bus stop every day and I think he fancies me! How do I find out?) we think it rather silly, and take it into school for the other girls to devour the comic strip stories, hidden under the desk tops, as the mistresses are also extremely scornful of this pulp fiction. "We ought to *look* like those girls though," says Susie doubtfully.

Mom has indeed conceded that we should no longer dress alike. Instead of the Co-op, she now takes us to Gear Cellar in C&A. She will not run to Chelsea Girl, which she disapproves of, and we gaze wistfully through the door into the exciting dark interior. I do manage to sneak in and buy two chain belts, gold for me and silver for Susie. Our dresses are shorter, our trousers wider. We eagerly embrace the fashions of the 1970s: flared trousers, tank tops, suede coats and midi skirts. Susie even crochets herself an orange and white poncho. The glamorous clothes of the 1960s seem a long way behind us.

There are few concessions at school to being a teenager. We are allowed to remove the bibs from our pinafores, probably because we are (embarrassingly) growing busts. The size of these is a huge talking point and Mrs Garrett, Domestic Science, gives us a lecture on wearing makeup (banned in school, but there is no doubt her powder and lipstick are immaculate). This is followed by a talk on being a Gracious Hostess, water lily napkins and flower arrangements, which none of us really do at home.

There is nothing we can do about our hair, as school is very strict on neatly brushed and tied back hair, but at the weekend we let our long hair hang free, with our noses peeking out from under the centre parting. For years, we have washed our hair in the sink on a Friday night, and gone round with it dripping down our backs. Now we have brand new hair dryers to dry it with. School also insists on low-heeled strap or lace up shoes, but at the weekend we stagger around on our wedgies and platform sole boots. Tights have replaced socks.

The little money we have, from birthdays and Christmases, is spent on the purchase of singles, which we dance to enthusiastically, playing them on Mom and Dad's new stereo Music Centre. They are better off now that Mom is back at work and Dad has his pools round. "What a racket," says Dad wincing, as we dance to T Rex, Sweet, the Bay City Rollers and Donny Osmond. He says the same when we put *Top of the Pops* on. He can't say the same of Radios Caroline and Luxembourg, as we listen to them on our transistor radios at night, under the bedclothes, with ear plugs in. Mom's radio is tuned permanently to the brand new Radio Two, but she does switch it to Radio One in the morning, so we can listen to Tony Blackburn and School Cool.

The big discussion at school is whether you like The Osmonds or The Jackson Five. It seems sad that all the great groups of the Sixties are gone – The Beatles, Gerry and the Pacemakers, Herman's Hermits and the Swinging Blue Jeans. Mom and Dad still have a complete collection of all their records, which is now relegated to the loft, and replaced with LPs of Frank Sinatra,

Ella Fitzgerald, Perry Como and Tony Bennett. Anyway, at least Tom Jones and Shirley Bassey are still going strong.

At Lucas's Great Hampton Street, Mom saves into something called the Make Up Chance, she puts in so much a week and every so often somebody from B6 assembly gets all the pot to spend at Snape's the Chemist opposite. One evening, she arrives home looking very pleased with herself. "I spent it on you!" With a flourish she gives me a carrier bag; in it are two lipsticks, one pale pink (my favourite colour), and one orange (her favourite colour). There is a Max Factor foundation, Pure Genius in a plastic tube, a little round cardboard box with a tiny puff called Bourjois Rouge, and a mascara in a little plastic case with a brush inside. She shows me how to spit on the cake of mascara to apply the mascara. "It's not *fair*," grumbles Susie.

Our first efforts at using this make up make us look rather like clowns and I, hopefully, borrow a book from the library with helpful illustrations on applying makeup. Mom gives me her Chance in future and Susie accompanies me to Snape's on Great Hampton Street. It's a lovely old fashioned chemist's with glass doors to its cupboards, staff in white overalls, and it smells glorious.

In truth, I would rather spend this money at Boots. They have a special range of makeup for teenagers called 17, and this range has things for *spots*. I have always had nice clear skin and then one Saturday morning I wake up and count six spots on my face. They don't go away despite all my best efforts with the products of 17, or Cathy and Claire's suggestions to drink water and avoid chocolate.

Another uncomfortable side effect of being a teenager is puppy fat. This also seems to come overnight and I am not the only one from school suffering with it. Susie is all right because, to my horror, she is actually growing taller than me and can take it. I remain short. "She'll have a growth spurt," say my aunts confidently (but I don't). Wild rumours circulate the school about weight loss using sulphur tablets and Ex-Lax. These are frowned upon by the mistresses, especially when Mr Wilcox the porter complains that the toilets are clogged up.

Mom stirs herself from her reveries to announce that I now need a bra, which announcement sends Susie off into hysterics. We trail off to Marks & Spencer and C&A, where I acquire a white bra edged with pink frills and a pink one covered with white flowers. Now undressing for PE in the changing rooms is even more of a horror; I am not one of those confident girls who compares bust sizes.

But worse is to come. One Thursday night, Mom is ironing while we watch *Top of the Pops*. She is having one of her post Nan's death depressions as we can see from her face, and we are very careful. Dad comes in. He looks very serious and his high colour is brick red. "There's something I have to tell you," he says gently. He launches into a stumbling explanation of periods. We are struck dumb with horror. Looking at Mom's face, I realise she has opted out of doing this, and Dad has included Susie as a two for the price of one, so he doesn't have to do this twice.

"So you see," he concludes, "you mustn't go with a boy. You might have a baby."

Pause – there is an uncomfortable silence.

"I wish I had been born a boy," I say at last.

Mom laughs bitterly. "I wish you had!" she says, and walks out of the room.

Indeed, a few months after, I do feel faint at school. I barely make it home, and stagger up to the toilet, where I am appalled to find blood on my knickers. I collapse onto my bed while Susie peers round the door anxiously. When Mom and Dad get in, Dad makes me a cup of tea and gives me an aspirin, Mom supplies a pink lace sanitary belt (the colour is a consolation) and a towel with loops on. "Be careful with boys now," she says firmly.

It is probably because of this that Dad not long after shows us how to throw a punch. He did lightweight boxing as a boy and in the Royal Marines; indeed, Aston is famous for its boxers and boxing clubs. It's *the* working class sport. "Now if a boy tries it on with you, just throw this punch." He is impressed with the fact that I do it with my left fist, "That's a southpaw!" It's because my left eye is stronger than my right, and I feel more confident. That Christmas, Dad buys us a darts board (his presents to us tend to be what he would have liked to get as a child) and soon I am throwing darts with my left hand also. But we don't get the chance to throw a punch at the youth club.

Of course, this subject should have been covered at school, but Miss Beechill, who teaches biology, had only told us blithely about the sex lives of rabbits and earthworms, which was very confusing. Wild rumours sweep the Lower Fifth. *Lady Chatterley's Lover* in a much thumbed edition is passed around and held to be very dull. Much more exciting is a book one of the girls finds under her Dad's pillow, *Doctors' Wives*.

Miss Beechill is replaced in the O Level stream by the younger Mrs Eagleton. One morning, she bends over her desk and says mysteriously, "Girls, what do you know about human reproduction?" The answer is, nothing really.

Following this, still in our science overalls, we are herded into the Lecture Theatre and bemusedly watch a silent cartoon film in which a stick man and a stick woman do strange things to each other, and produce a stick baby (a twiglet?). "I think I'll just become a nun," says one of the Catholic girls.

Another horror is in store for us. In my final year at William Cowper, I was sent to Mr Lacey's, the school dentist in Aston, to have excess teeth removed. "It was horrible," I say to Susie. "He stuck a mask on my face and pumped gas into me, but I wasn't really asleep, I could feel all the extractions, except I had a nightmare. Mr Lacey was chasing after me in his white coat, and he had a dagger. Oh, and when I woke up, the blood was everywhere, like a Hammer horror film." Susie, awaiting the same process, bursts into tears and Dad is *furious*.

With all my excess teeth removed, it is time to go on a waiting list for Birmingham's Dental Hospital, and sure enough I am summoned there in late 1970, so I have to take a day off school. Mom is still subject to depression, so Dad writes the note, takes a half day off work and accompanies me there. The Dental Hospital is situated opposite St Chad's Cathedral and is a large tower block like building. A dentist in a white coat tuts angrily over my teeth. "A brace for those sticking up front teeth," he says, "and to pull the rest back into line. Also, her teeth are yellow, brush three times a day with Colgate."

Dad, whose own teeth like the rest of the family's, are yellow despite brushing three times a day with Colgate, nods eagerly and does not say that the yellowing family teeth are due to generations of neglect of working class teeth, only remedied since the birth of the NHS. Or that some of the women who worked in munitions during the wars had teeth removed when their gums were poisoned by acid. There follows an hour of sheer agony in the dentist chair, while a huge metal brace is fitted over my teeth. I am appalled when I look in the mirror. I already have spots, puppy fat and greasy hair and now I have a mouthful of metal. It is unlikely any boy at the bus stop will ever want to ask me out. "There's a little key at the side, we'll turn it when she comes here," directs the dentist.

Susie has a fit of hysterics when she sees my brace and the next day I wake up with a very sore jaw, which continues for days. Mom is actually interested in the fact that I can hardly eat and serves up soup – Campbell's tomato. "It's agony," I say to Susie, "and it'll be you next." At which she bursts into tears again, and Dad comes storming in again. I escape to my room, and reflect that we are not the happy family we were before Nan died. Susie and I now have regular arguments and some of these are complete with hair pullings and kicking. This of course makes Dad mad, and as for Mom, she has retreated completely into anger and depression. Our family is indeed like the turbulent Seventies.

There are, of course, some nicer bits to becoming a teenager. We are, for example, allowed to watch whatever we want on the telly (Mom and Dad do not practise censorship). Secretly, we still hanker after *Watch with Mother, Captain Scarlet and the Mysterons*, and *Jackanory*, and as in fact we have one telly with three channels, we just end up watching what Mom and Dad watch: *Z Cars, Dixon of Dock Green, Opportunity Knocks*, and *Doomwatch*. And as Dad still likes Westerns, we all gather round to watch *Lancer* and *The High Chaparral*. This last is a special favourite as there is somebody in there for all of us: Manolito for me, Billy Blue for my sister, Uncle Buck for Mom, and Victoria ("Isn't she beautiful?") for Dad. In fact, we like it so much that we get the annual for Christmas, along with the *Match of the Day Annual for Boys*. This last is because we still watch *MOTD* with Dad (and we enjoy the stirring new theme tune), and he needs to dispel our appalling ignorance of the offside rule. Our acquaintance with England began with the 1966 World Cup, and it's been downhill all the way since then in 1970 and 1974. It's sad to say farewell to Sir Alf Ramsey, one of Dad's heroes (with Harold) of the 1960s.

Comedies are something we all enjoy: *Dad's Army, Man About the House, Some Mothers Do 'Ave 'Em, Steptoe and Son* and *Till Death Us Do Part*. Christmas finds us all gathered around the telly for the Morecambe and Wise Christmas Show. Morecambe and Wise *are* the Seventies.

Susie and I still have our own favourites: *The Double Deckers, The Banana Splits, Ask Aspel* and *Points of View*. But sometimes I think of *Watch with Mother* on the radio and telly wistfully.

It's the same with my books.

I have a complete bookcase of books by Enid Blyton and books about ponies, ballet and boarding schools. They're also the books I borrowed whenever we went to Birchfield Library. Now we have moved, Dad thinks it is time to switch to the library in Birmingham City Centre, the Victorian Reference Library.

Susie isn't interested – she doesn't choose to read anymore, but plays card games and board games such as Cluedo, Buckaroo and Monopoly with Kim. Kim and Susie are drifting away from me. The age gap is showing.

But Dad still likes his film and history books, so he takes me along. There's no children's library as there was in Birchfield and I drift around the bookshelves looking for something to read. There's very little, so I take along my reading list from Mrs Davies, English, and take a tentative step into the Adult Library, where the shelves are very tall. It has a beautiful spiral staircase in the middle. Using my list, I select three titles (I have only three library tickets): *The Scarlet Pimpernel*, *Pride and Prejudice*, and an historical novel by Jean Plaidy called *Flaunting Extravagant Queen*, which I pick because I like the picture of Marie Antoinette on the cover. In fact, over the next two years, I read every Jean Plaidy in the library.

Clutching my books, on the way home, I say to Dad, "I like that library."

"It's going to be demolished," he says.

I'm shocked. "Demolished? But it's lovely!"

"It's part of the rebuilding of the city," he says.

The rebuilding of Birmingham, in the 1970s, by City Planner Sir Herbert Manzoni and architect John Madin, is now controversial. It is forgotten that they were trying to create a new Birmingham in which we could live, travel and work. But for many of us, it meant loss, as entire streets, schools, shops, and cinemas were demolished – Birmingham's Victorian heritage. Some of the buildings are exciting – Mom takes us to the opening of the Queensway in 1971, and we see the Queen from a distance. Not far from there is the Kennedy mosaic, opened in 1968. Spaghetti Junction opens in 1972, and the Rotunda in 1965 ("Both built by the Irish," says my Dad.)

But some of it is sad.

Guildford Street is long gone, hidden under a new housing estate. The small shops along Newtown Row and the market, once bustling, are all gone also. Most of the cinemas are now shut, or Bingo Halls. Then there is the saddest loss of all.

In 1972, Dad takes us to see the demolition of William Cowper School. It is to be replaced by a modern, flat topped building. There is quite a festive atmosphere down at the school, which soon dispels as the bulldozer moves in and the bell tower falls. Then, as it moves into the school, we can see the arched roof fall, and the balconies, and the classrooms.

I tug at Dad's sleeve.

"Let's go!" I beg.

We walk home, even Dad seeming subdued.

"Nobody cares about working class heritage," he says at last. "It's not just about big houses and palaces. Something should have been kept of our houses, factories, cinemas, shops and schools."

I walk to where 37 Guildford Street used to stand. Our house was opposite Geach Street, and they haven't built on that bit. It's just a patch of derelict land. I remember Dad posting the keys back through the letterbox on the day we left, and wonder whether if I dug down, I would find them.

The back to backs are gone, though Dad says there are some on Hurst Street, where he goes up to George the Tailor for Repairs and Alterations. They are acting as shops, that's why they haven't been demolished.

To me, the new concrete Birmingham is ugly, as my school uniform seems ugly. I feel ugly, with my puppy fat, spots and newly greasy hair. Mom and Dad think our pop records are ugly and wince during *Pick of the Pops*. The Newtown estate is ugly, all concrete and metal. Even the few flowers are scentless, unattractive roses with thorns – to stop us from picking them. The Seventies in fact, so far, seem a very ugly decade.

I need something to do.

Susie and Kim don't play with me anymore. We can still go out together to ride all over the estate on our bikes and roller skates, but then they retreat to Kim's bedroom to play Buckaroo. Our dolls, our toys, have been relegated to the loft.

The cinema of the 1970s is a poor affair. Our local cinemas – the Newtown Palace, the Villa Cross, the Orient – are now bingo halls or boarded up. Trips to the Gaumont or Birmingham Odeon are for school expeditions, though Mom and Dad do now go there for James Bond films. Lesley and I meet one Saturday to see *On the Buses* at the Perry Barr Clifton, which is a new cinema for me, but most of the films are rated X or A, which means we need an accompanying adult. We can only go to U films, even though we are teenagers.

At school, Mrs Davies invites me to be in the Chorus of the school production of *Murder in the Cathedral*. Learning my part, rehearsals, and being fitted for my costume take up a lot of my time, but sadly Dad falls asleep during the performance as he thinks it is so boring. *The Beacon* school magazine, however, is greatly impressed with our screaming when the Archbishop is murdered.

I still go on Wednesdays to the Hazeltree School of Dance with Julie Lane, though Susie has stopped going. Julie and I are in a show, but I'm beginning to realise that I'm never going to be a ballerina.

Lynne Atkins invites us to a disco at her local youth club. This is very exciting, and we treat ourselves (to Mom's horror), to new sets of hot pants. Mine are blue and white and Susie's are bright orange. But when we get there, we are too shy to dance. Some girls dance in circles around their bags, but the few boys there hang around the edge of the floor.

The one day Lesley says to me, "Meet me in Birmingham on Saturday?" I stare at her in surprise, I have never been into Birmingham without Mom and suddenly I realise that I can. "I'll get the bus down the Walsall Road," she continues, "and I'll meet you outside the Midland Educational." When I meet her there, after catching the No 51 in, we are identifiable by our blue school macs, which are the best coats we have.

We have a wonderful time; we explore the Midland Educational, we ride the escalators up to the top floor of Lewis's and down again. We catch the lift up to the top floor in Rackham's, we browse the record collection in WH Smith's, and the books in Hudson's of New Street, and we have lemonade and fancy cakes in Drucker's pastry shop in the Great Western Arcade. I venture at last into the dark and fascinating exterior of Chelsea Girl. The city is our new playground.

When we part, she says, "See you here again next week. I'll bring Jennie." It's the beginning of a love affair with the City Centre that I have to this day.

7

The Wonderful World of Work

1972–1974

It all starts because I need some money. I am going to be in a show with the Hazeltree School of Dance and I need to buy some items but I haven't got the money. Pocket money is not part of working class culture, every penny has its place. Mom is still paid with a pay packet on a Thursday, but since he was promoted to foreman, Dad has a bank account. He had to go to Lloyd's on the Queensway to open it because they are open on a Saturday and he works Monday to Friday. He doesn't think much of having to write himself a cheque for money, but there's no doubt the cheques are useful for paying the rent, as we don't have a rent collector anymore (£5 a week, whereas Guildford Street was 15 shillings a week). Mom can also drop cheques in at the MEB and British Gas instead of having a payment book. But, like everyone else we know, Dad does not have an overdraft and he does not have a credit card.

We are still not very well off despite their working, Mom's *Burlington* catalogue, and Dad's pools round. It's because they suddenly got fed up of doing without. They have ordered a new three-piece suite and some beds and wardrobes. Then there is the bigger, though still black and white, telly and the music centre. And the fridge-freezer, which means Mom doesn't have to shop every day and we can make ice cubes for our drinks. All these are on Hire Purchase from shops in the precinct, and Mom has a collection of payment books.

Then there is the phone. After Nan died, we had such trouble getting in touch with each other that we all decided to get telephones. There is a large telegraph pole on New John Street West and Dad puts our name down on the GPO waiting list. One day, I come home from school and there in the hall is a cream coloured dialling phone. It has a label on it, informing us to dial 100 for the operator, and 999 for the emergency services. Of course, I instantly phone Lesley to see if she is at home and Dad is soon rationing time on the phone, especially when we discover *Dial a Disc*, the *YouTube* of its time; there are threats of locks. Dad does dial the weather occasionally, but Mom doesn't call *Dial a Recipe*, she gave up baking when Nan died.

All this costs money, and there isn't any spare.

On the way back from the Community Centre, I dawdle through the precinct, reading the notices outside Dillon's. And there it is! *'Boys and Girls wanted for early morning and evening paper rounds'*. This is the solution to my problem, I can earn enough money to buy what I need!

I run home and pour out my story to Mom and Dad. They look at each other. Dad clears his throat, "We wouldn't be keen on you going out early morning and late evening... it's not safe... I'll give you the money for what you need." This is very disappointing. After the show, in which I have a very minor part, I give up the school of dance, much to Julie Lane's disappointment, because unlike life in a Lorna Hill, I am never suddenly going to be chosen for the Royal Ballet School (*"No training, but she's a natural! A miracle!"*)

I also follow up a couple of advertisements at Dillon's for babysitting, but when I get to whatever house it is on the estate, the job has always just gone. When I am fourteen, I am uncomfortably aware that at my age Mom and Dad were earning and not just that, they were earning in factories that bombs were being dropped on. I, on the other hand, am only just about to enter the O Level stream.

The general idea amongst the working classes is to get the children out of school and into work as soon as possible, to augment the family income. Possibly not at the age of eight anymore, but certainly earlier than sixteen and the Grammar School that my parents are so proud of is seen as a waste of time. "You should get them out of that school," says my Great Aunt Min to Mom. Mom tosses her head, "It'll pay off in the end. They'll get jobs as teachers, or in libraries. They'll be white collar, not blue collar."

One summer, I see an advertisement in the *Birmingham Evening Mail*; fourteen year olds are invited to get work experience by working for the Birmingham Show, apply in your own writing to the Council. I dutifully do so.

The Birmingham Show is held every year over the August Bank Holiday. 1970 is the first year the Show will be in Perry Park, it has been in Handsworth

Park before. The Show has Dog Shows and show jumping, it has a pop-up pub called the Barleycorn, a flower show in a tent, a fair, as well as a pop group, performers and it concludes with fireworks. It also has food and drink stalls and I receive a typewritten letter asking me to attend for an interview in the City Catering Department in Summer Lane, where a very fierce lady interviews me, but it's alright because I receive a letter telling me I have got the job. I will be working two days over the Bank Holiday, and of course as I haven't got a bank account, I can call into Summer Lane the week after and collect my pay packet.

I duly report to my stall on August Bank Holiday Saturday and I am issued with a polyester overall and cap. There is a till, but I haven't been trained on it, so I am mainly serving the public. It seems a very odd menu: all we serve is pork pies, in plastic packets. The drinks are called Max Pax, water is added to powder from a scalding urn and there are three only: coffee, tea, and hot chocolate. I can have as many drinks as I like, but I don't drink coffee and the tea tastes rather as I imagine Dettol to be like, so I exist for two days on the healthy diet of very hot chocolate and pork pies.

The consolation of this rather odd employment is that I am allowed to wander around the park after and watch the fireworks and on Sunday they are giving the flowers away, so I get a very nice bunch for Mom. Also, I have my first Reference.

When Mom was fourteen, Nan, by then a war widow with five children to feed, said to her, "Go out and don't come back till you find a job." Mom had just finished at Lozells Girls' Secondary; she had a glowing Leaving Certificate, which I have still. She was so good at mathematics – she can add her supermarket bill up in her head – they wanted her to go to Aston Technical School and do bookkeeping, but she couldn't do that, she had to earn. We don't have careers in the working classes, you see. We have jobs.

In the same way, when I am fifteen, Mom suddenly says, "Go into Birmingham City Centre and don't come back till you have a Saturday job." It is Saturday morning and I am looking forward to *The Banana Splits* and *Grandstand*. I might go up to the library on the bus, and get myself a Jean Plaidy or a Dorothy L. Sayers (detective fiction is my new passion). Dad is where he is every Saturday morning, under the A60. It is a rust bucket, it needs constant maintenance, and he can't afford a new car or a garage. "British cars going to pot," he grumbles. "In 20 years, Japan and Germany will lead the field."

Nevertheless, he is thinking of taking up golf to go with his management aspirations, and is investigating the municipal courses. Johnnie Murray is going to play with him. Very soon, they are spending every Saturday on a Birmingham municipal golf course, and talking wistfully of joining Great Barr private golf club.

Susie is off with Kim Harrison.

This means I am uncomfortably alone with Mom, because she is very bad tempered on Saturdays, it is Wash Day. At Guildford Street, she washed by hand on a Monday with Nan in the brewhouse, and Susie and I put the clothes through the mangle, before they pegged them on the line. Now she has a hoover twin tub. It is not very good, but it is all they can afford (it is also on Hire Purchase), and it is as bad tempered as Mom. It is extremely noisy and when it goes into spin, it dances around all over the kitchen, pursued by Mom who is screaming at the top of her voice (it is the first time I have realised that she can swear). Dad has promised to buy her a new machine on Hire Purchase as soon as the present round of HP is finished.

So maybe getting out of the house might not be a bad thing. Moreover, she is equally bad tempered once the washing is over, and she puts her hair up in her brand new but extremely uncomfortable Carmen electric rollers, which steam gently on her head.

I go upstairs and change into a C&A dress, and put on my school mac as it is my smartest coat. I brush my hair and decide to leave it hanging loose, with a hairband holding it back from my face and I anxiously apply my makeup. As my dress is white and green, I add some green eye shadow which doesn't really go with my pink lipstick. I shoulder my bag and trail out of the house to the bus stop on Newtown Row, outside the Newtown Palace (now a bingo hall). I sulkily reflect that the two shop stewards don't seem to mind that their daughter will be working a six day week.

I have no idea how to look for a Saturday job.

I suppose I may as well walk around all the shops and ask somebody – anybody – if there are any jobs going. I start with my favourites, but automatically exclude Chelsea Girl, where the girls are all thin with long tossing hair and clear skin, and Lewis's, Grey's and Rackham's, because they are so posh. I stare at the windows of Dorothy Perkins and Richard Shops without daring to go in. The Midland Educational, Hudson's Bookshop, WH Smith's and Boots are not hiring. I walk around, looking for advertisements; for somebody as shy as myself, it is agonising.

The last shop I get to, on the High Street, before I can thankfully get the bus home, is Littlewood's. This is not a shop I know well. Mom thinks it is a rather dreary old lady shop, and it has nothing for me to go in for, but I go in and say to the first girl I see, "Are there any Saturday jobs going, please?" She looks me up and down, "I think Personnel are in. I'll take you up." She takes me to the back of the store, where there are some lift doors. We ride up, and she punches a number into a keypad on a door which says *STAFF ONLY*. There is an office beyond it marked *Personnel*, and a lady sitting at a typewriter. "Lady looking for a job," says my mentor, as I thank her.

The lady from Personnel is cool but kind. They have jobs she says, but I need to do tests in English and Maths; I should be all right, because I am a Grammar School Girl. My nerves are now so bad that I completely mess up the Maths test. "Please let me try again!" I beg. She relents and I am much calmer, and pass both.

"Start next Saturday," she says briskly. "Be here for a quarter to nine and come to Personnel for your overall. It's from quarter to nine till quarter past six, and it's a pound a day, paid in arrears." I go home and tell Mom and Dad, who seem quite pleased ("apart from it being such a boring shop," says Mom), and Susie is very envious.

On Monday, Dad has to send in a letter to school to ask formal permission for me to have a Saturday job. Lots of the girls do, but I have to go and see Miss Sargeant, now Headmistress. This is an unnerving experience, involving waiting outside her study for a traffic light to turn green, and then crossing a wide expanse of floor to stand in front of her desk. However, permission is given.

The next Saturday, Dad gives me a lift into town because to be honest, if I pay two lots of bus fare, my wages will be wiped out. He drops me outside Littlewood's. I am sick with nerves, but daren't show it. The store is not open yet, but a caretaker is standing inside the glass doors and lets me in. I make my way to the lift and up to Personnel. The staff area is full of girls on their way down, all chatting and confident and beautifully made up. I feel worse than ever.

The Personnel lady issues me with a locker and key and a navy blue overall. My heart sinks as navy blue is the school uniform colour and the overall shows up all my lumps and bumps. Her eyes sweep over me, "Hair tied back," she says. Luckily, I have an elastic band in my pocket and I manage to twist my hair band over it, like a ribbon.

I fill in some more forms in my office, and then we hear some pips over a loudspeaker. "Nine o'clock and opening," says the Personnel lady briskly. "You'll hear those on the shop floor at break and dinner time. You have two fifteen minute breaks and an hour for lunch. You have a staff discount –

twenty per cent off anything you buy, show your badge at the till." I can't see that I will want to buy anything from them.

She shows me the staff canteen which smells of chips and stewed tea, rather like the British Home Stores café, and then takes me down in the lift, right down to the basement. "This is Miss Orme, your supervisor. I'll leave you with her." She nods and goes off.

Dressed in the same ugly navy blue uniform, Miss Orme is very young, very pretty, very well made up and very slender, and she can't be much older than I am. She seems pleasant, gives me a staff badge, and tells me I am on first break. Then she leads me over to a counter. "This is your counter. Julie is on it during the week. I'll show you what to do."

The basement at Littlewood's is dedicated to ladies wear and the café, which I can smell from my counter. The counters are long, four-sided with two racks and have a small entrance to the inner area, which has rows of shelves of boxes with excess stock. I stare aghast at my counter. It is ladies' underwear, but not of a type I have ever seen before; they are in fact bloomers. They are bloomers for old ladies, made out of thick cotton in a variety of amazing shades of purple, orange and yellow, and the size starts at X Large and moves up through XXL to XXXL. They are displayed in little heaps across the counters.

"Now you need to keep the stock tidy, and replenish any that's sold. Anything you are asked for and we haven't got, you can go up and look in the stockroom. Breaks at ten and three, and dinner at twelve. I'm around if needed," says Miss Orme and walks off.

I begin my endless, endless perambulations round the counter. It's a relief when the pips sound for break and I go up to the canteen, but I sit dumbly, not knowing any of the other girls. Dinner at twelve is an hour for egg and chips.

In the afternoon, I have my first problem. "I want lime green in XXXL," says an older lady. Of course, we have every colour in that size apart from green. I look around for Miss Orme. "Take the lift up to the stockroom, and ask one of the men to help you, while I mind the counter," she advises.

Something else I don't know how to do. I take the lift, an iron cage, to the very top floor and look around desperately for help. It is full of very tall shelves of stock. At length, I see a man working in an aisle. "I need ladies' bloomers," I whisper, crimson with embarrassment, but he doesn't seem to care and directs me to an aisle where it is very dark, and I spend fifteen minutes crawling over it and up ladders to find the elusive bloomers. By the time I get back down, the customer has gone.

"She said she was going to the Home Stores," says Miss Orme crossly. "You need to be quicker, Miss Holte (we are always addressed by our surnames), and you need to do a stock edit every Saturday morning to make sure you have everything." By three o'clock tea break, I am totally demoralised as I drink my stewed tea, and then at three-thirty, Mom and Susie turn up.

Susie has been envious at my first job, but now goes off into hysterics at the sight of my counter. I am resolved that I will never let Jennie and Lesley visit me here. "It's not the most becoming overall," says Mom, "and your hair just doesn't look good like that. Well, we're off to C&A. I suppose I should really buy something here," and she looks around doubtfully and gives up. "See you at the bus stop... "

I brighten at the thought of going home. But when the pips sound at six o'clock, nobody leaves. "We can't go till cashing up is done," explains Miss Orme. The tills are still manual and cashing up takes some time, so it is in fact six-thirty before I can crawl off to the 33 bus stop, under Nathan's the Jeweller's clock, Corporation Street, where Mom and Susie are waiting impatiently. Not a good day.

Week two is even worse and I have been dreading it all week despite Jennie and Lesley's eager questions. Miss Orme is waiting on the shop floor with one of the permanent staff; they do one Saturday in two. Her name is Julie and she has a face like thunder. "I told Miss Orme to look at my counter on Monday, it was a terrible mess, I had to clear it all up!" I mutter apologies, my face scarlet. I want to say it would be nice if somebody had shown me what to do, but I daren't. And also I want to say that school hasn't prepared me in any way for this.

"You can spend a bit of time today with Julie showing you what to do," interposes Miss Orme (my heart sinks). "In the meantime, as it's her day on, I want you to go on the till." Tills are scattered all over the shop floor, one at each station (in order to stop us chatting). I have about five minutes of instruction, and then it's me and my till.

In 1972, tills are not electric. It is an old fashioned manual till, and I have to key in the amount spent, which then pops up on a display of tabs, and opens the till, so I can take the money and give the change. It does not add up for you. Putting in one pair of bloomers at seven and sixpence is easy enough, with two shillings and sixpence change from a ten shilling note, but of course one of my first customers comes up with ten balls of wool at one and sixpence each. I do quick calculations in my head, and quote them the price before I ring it up. I decide I need a notebook and pencil, and will ask

Personnel for one at break. The prices are relatively simple, but the halfpennies throw me a bit. There are no credit card transactions, because very few people have cards. It is all cash.

There is one bright spot in the day. When I go up for dinner on (second) break, the girls are queuing outside Personnel, for pay slips, and I join them. "H for Holte," mutters the Personnel lady, searching a large box. It is full of little plastic bags stapled at the top with a brown label. I feel I am here under false pretences, that there will be nothing for me. And then, with a flourish, she hands me a brown packet with Miss G. Holte and a number written on it. "That's your payroll number… You need it whenever you fill in an overtime sheet."

I scuttle off to the canteen, find a table and gloat over my payslip. It contains one grubby pound note. That afternoon, I have to spend some time with Julie, who is pretty but rather belligerent. She shows me exactly how she thinks the counter should be tidied. Then it's back on the till and at six o'clock Miss Orme shows me how to cash up, and mercifully, it balances. The money goes into a canvas bag, and we till assistants have to take it up to Personnel to put in the safe, and then at last I can crawl to the bus stop. I have never been so exhausted in my life.

I stay at Littlewood's for nearly two years. I don't bother to look for another job as I have some sort of misplaced sense of loyalty to them, and things do get slightly better. For one, they replace the hated navy blue overall with a new, lighter blue checked one, which is a bit of an improvement. I never get over the tiredness of circling the counter all day, and most of us sneak into the inner area and take a small rest on a shelf or on the floor. I don't know if they notice this, but one Saturday, we have new counters with no inner area. The stock is in drawers on the outside; now there is no respite from the endless circling.

The staff discount is of little use to me; I buy one item in the two years I am there, an orange and white cotton frock for one pound nineteen and sixpence, which my mother claims is too small and girlish for me. Possibly due to Julie's rather angry tuition, I become an expert on cleaning and displaying my counter and replenishing the stock. So good, in fact, that Julie insists that only I can work her counter out of all the Saturday Girls. Praise indeed.

Word of this reaches Miss Orme, now Mrs Randle (honeymoon in Spain, much to our interest, the birth of the package holiday abroad) and she recommends me for overtime. This is usually over the summer holidays but I am also asked to go in at Christmas, there is no Sunday opening, so this, to my annoyance, means going in after school to do a couple of hours till closing time. Now I really know what tiredness is. Littlewood's is very dreary at

Christmas, with no special merchandise, and I am usually sent to circulate the racks with winter coats on. But Town looks lovely with its Christmas lights.

I become an expert on the tills. I have learnt more about adding up and multiplication than I have ever done at school, and am rather sorry when they replace the old manual tills with electric ones. I also notice that all the capable supervisors are female, but all the managers are male, and I wonder about this.

Of course, the best thing is that I now have a pound to spend. Mom and Dad insist that I put some of it in my Post Office Savings account at the Newtown Precinct Post Office, but I still have enough to trail off to Boots and buy myself a 17 lipstick, or to Hudson's Bookshop for a Noel Streatfeild paperback. And when I do overtime, I have more than a pound to spend.

Lynne Atkins is now working at British Home Stores, which Mom thinks is better than Littlewood's because of its lighting department. If there is a film on at the Odeon, the Gaumont or the Queensway, we meet after work, have something to eat at the Tennessee Pancake House and go to the pictures.

I make three friends at Littlewood's, all Saturday Girls, and all Grammar School Girls like myself. There is in fact a bit of a standoff between us and the permanent staff, who think we are la di da. Hence Julie's initial enmity. Bernadette is Irish, she has long black hair, blue eyes, and the most beautiful skin as my Mom says admiringly when she calls in, as she does every Saturday and sees Bernie sitting haughtily at the till, looking around. Bernie and I drift around the shops at lunch time, and I finally pluck up the courage to enter Chelsea Girl with her, Richard Shops, Dorothy Perkins and Miss Selfridge. Alas, one Saturday, Bernie is told to work in the café which she refuses to do; it is not her job. She walks out and I never see her again.

"That girl could be a shop steward and lead a walk out," says Dad approvingly. I daren't tell Dad that following Bernie's departure, I was ordered to go and work in the café. I haven't got Bernie's guts and I daren't give up my job; I heard Mom telling Auntie Margaret how proud she was that I had one, and how grown up it made me look. So I spend a miserable afternoon cleaning tables and loading trays.

Cassie is my next friend. She is tall, blonde, slender and confident, and best of all she turns out to be the daughter of Ray Cooper, who used to run the Newsagent's on Newtown Road. It's a lovely link with the past, when the present seems so ugly and miserable.

Ann is my last friend there, in my last year. Ann is more like me, plain with straight, tied back hair. But Ann doesn't seem to mind this as I do. She tells me she is working hard at school to get into University, and she wants to go to Nottingham. This is something I have never considered, but I think I know now that I am not heading for a career in hospitality or retail.

In the meantime, Susie has started her round of Saturday jobs. Her first job is at Edwards fruit and veg in the precinct, and it should be great, because she can walk there. But the manager is nasty to her and it's like the old days at school: Mom goes down and gives him a piece of her mind. He slinks off, terrified by her fiery wrath and flashing eyes; Mom tosses her head and takes Susie over to Halford's under Inkerman Tower, and gets her a job there. Susie loves it, and Uncle Bertie Burke and Dad like it so much that they go in every Saturday and buy discount stock. Then disaster strikes, the age of employment rises and Halford's regretfully gives Susie her cards. "When I think we started at fourteen!" fumes Mom.

Susie has to wait several months and then she goes to Woolworth's on Soho Road after school, and asks for a Saturday job there. I am a bit envious as Woolworth's is more exciting than Littlewood's, but to her annoyance Susie is placed every week on the cheese counter. She hates cheese.

I think, however, that it is obvious that we are not headed for a career in retail and one Friday night, when I am bracing myself for another dreary Saturday with the giant bloomers and the old ladies, Dad says suddenly, "Why don't you try for a Saturday job in the library?" Well, that sounds good. There is a Council vacancies advertisement in the *Mail* every Thursday night, but on Dad's advice I write a letter addressed to Personnel at Birmingham Central Library; this is in fact the new Library, which opened in 1973.

Back comes a typewritten form for me to fill in. There is a waiting list. I fill in the form and hesitate over *Reasons for Wanting Employment*. "Because," says Dad sternly, "your present intention is to one day work professionally in the Library Service, and this will provide much needed experience." This is the first I have ever heard of it. But it sounds good.

Only a few months later a typewritten letter arrives from Personnel, Birmingham Library Services saying can I please report for an interview at the Library. I'm less nervous now than I used to be. After some anxious arrangements made by telephone, I go up after school one day in one of my Miss Selfridge dresses and my best pink coat. I am interviewed by a lady from Personnel and a lady called Joan Billingham. The interview goes well – the only test is to put some books in order on a trolley, which is easy, and shortly after that I receive a letter offering me a Saturday job at the Central Library. Mom and Dad are very impressed that I am now a Council employee. Prestige. "That is much more secure than industry," says Dad.

There are some changes in my employment. I will wear a badge, but do not have to wear a uniform. I begin at nine, but finish at five, so I'll have an hour to wander around Birmingham. The pay is five pounds a Saturday! It will be paid monthly and I need a bank account. I am sixteen, so I can have a bank account but Dad has to go with me to open it. All the banks in the precinct are closed on a Saturday, so he takes me to his own bank, Lloyd's on the Queensway, where I am terribly intimidated by the Manager in his dark three-piece suit, and his office of polished mahogany. I fill in various forms and promise to be a good customer. "It's a good way to start, in local government," smiles the Manager.

Having to write yourself a cheque for money is not so good (I feel nostalgic for my pay packet), but the Manager tells us about a new service coming in: a Cash Machine, where you can use a card and a number to withdraw cash. "Well, that's useful," says Dad, "as the banks are always closed when I come out of work." For good measure, he takes me over to the Halifax in Colmore Row to start a Savings Account with a little blue book. "Put money in every month," he directs.

I have to give a week's notice at Littlewood's, to the lady in Personnel whose name I have never found out. She gives me a satisfaction survey to fill in. I don't fill in what I really think, and say untruthfully that I have really enjoyed every minute of my two years' service. Besides, Mrs Randle, Julie and Ann are really distraught, so the week after I bring in a box of Quality Street for them all. "The best Saturday assistant ever," says Mrs Randle tearfully.

Well, that's something.

The new Birmingham Central Library opened in 1973. In fact, I would rather have been offered a job at one of the branches, like Birchfield or Aston, which are not so big, but everyone seems quite impressed. The library was designed by the architect John Madin, replacing the 1883 Victorian building, which has now been demolished. It is a part of the controversial City Council plan for the design of the Inner Ring Road, and they call its style Brutalist. In fact, it's just part and parcel of the ugly decade that the Seventies seems to be turning into.

I like it myself. I have been a member since it opened and was surprised that I no longer needed little blue or brown tickets to borrow books. Instead, I have an orange plastic card with little dots on it which is put in a slot on the counter and a bar pen reads codes inside the book.

As I have spent so much time in the library already, I am not at all nervous when Dad drops me off on my first morning. I am wearing what I think is a very cool dress from the Bull Ring Rag Market (two pounds) and my hair is swinging loose under a hair band (no rules on long hair). We enter a side door, where the porter is waiting, and I make my way up to the Lending Library. Joan is waiting for me; she gives me a staff badge and introduces me to the rest of the staff. "Tour of the building first," she says, "and counter this afternoon. Shadowing all day."

The new Central Library consists of two buildings, representing the two branches of Librarianship. One, looking out, represents Lending and has the Lending Library, the Children's Library, and Quick Reference or asking questions as we call it, where the staff patiently answer questions on bus timetables, local councillors, and MP surgeries. There is of course no Internet. All information comes from books, leaflets, pamphlets, posters and people. The other service in this part is the Audio Visual Library, which loans out slide collections and films, mainly on the history of Birmingham.

Linking this with the Reference Library, which is inverted, is a corridor with a café, elevators and lifts up to the staff area. Joan takes me up to the staff area and shows me the canteen, which is brand new, large and very pleasant. Then we pass into the Reference Area, taking the elevator down every floor. There are six floors of Reference – this is the biggest Reference Library in Europe – Fine Arts, Language and Literature (I brighten), Local Studies and Family History, Science (not so good), Music, and Social Sciences. These books are not for lending, and there is an enquiry desk on every floor with staff ready to help. There are hundreds of people sitting around in study areas. Some of the areas are women only.

There is a whole floor dedicated to a very exciting Music Library, full of records. "We don't just loan records," explains a staff member, "we've also got a lot of musical scores, say if someone is doing an operetta, and needs some. And if somebody rings up asking the name of a piece of music, they sing it for us, and then we go and find it out."

Joan also shows me the rolling stacks, huge rows of shelves opened with a handle on which excess books and collections are stored. On our way down to Lending, the elevator shudders to a halt. "This happens all the time," says Joan resignedly. She takes me into Lending, where I am based, and introduces me to all the staff. Lending has an In and Out desk, and it has an enquiry desk, and everything is fresh and bright and new.

I shadow a friendly girl called Shashi all day. Shashi, who has curly hair and wire rimmed glasses and wears trousers, shows me my shadowing timetable. I seem fated to run around at the behest of timetables. I work on the Returns counter and Issue Counter, inserting orange cards into the desk and reading bar codes with a pen. I take my trolley of books off into the library and shelve, making notes on what I want to borrow. I sit on the Enquiry Desk, watching the staff answer questions, and using a huge range of paper resources to do so; sometimes they have to make a phone call to answer a question. They also deal with enquiries by post. "Carefully, though," says Heather on Enquiries, bent over her brand new computer screen, "because of the IRA letter bomb campaign." A goose walks softly over my grave.

There are no pips – Joan tells us when our tea breaks and lunch break are, and we go to the canteen. All the men wear suits and the girls wear their own clothes – there are no overalls here, just a BCC staff badge. I'm a bit conscious of my handkerchief sleeved dress, bought for two pounds from the Bull Ring, and my cheap shoes from the Newtown Precinct. I do not look fashionable. I console myself with the fact that when I am paid, I will venture into Chelsea Girl and get some really teenage clothes.

The day finishes at five o'clock, so I've still got an hour to wander down New Street and into Hudson's Bookshop before I meet Mom at the bus stop. The pigeons are cooing in St Philip's Cathedral gardens, and swallows wheel over New Street.

Four weeks later, I get paid and at five pounds a day this is the most money I have ever had. My pay slip (not pay packet) is waiting for me in the staff area in Central Lending. My cheque book, speedbank card and number have been sent to me in the post, so at lunchtime I rush off to the nearest Lloyds Bank, and after a bit of anxious experimentation, draw out a pound with which I go to the Co-op and buy myself some clip on earrings. I am a worker. I am a wage earner. I work for the Council.

There is an exciting event just after I start. Joan says to me, "Do you want to come to the official opening of the library with Harold Wilson?" This is in 1974. Rather to Dad's surprise, Harold was re-elected with a very narrow margin in February 1974, after four years of a Heath government culminating in the Three Day Week and industrial unrest. "Of course," remarks Dad, "I always said that Harold was the only PM who could work with the Unions, and that the Unions would bring Ted Heath down. It should be Happy Days again. But Harold's lost his fire." And by this time, Dad is no longer a shop steward or a member of the Labour Party. He is in Management.

"But we opened last year!" I say to Joan.

"Yes, but this is the official opening, and I can get you a place."

This is all very exciting, especially since it will also be in the presence of Birmingham's first female Lord Mayor, so I mention it to Dad, who is also excited.

On a sunny day in January 1974, we all gather to watch Harold make a speech and unveil a plaque, then tour the building. He stops to talk to the Readers Adviser in Lending, and I watch him from a distance. The Central Library is now gone, but the plaque remains at the top of the new library of Birmingham, outside the Shakespeare Memorial Room.

I like the library so much that when Susie is sixteen and still at the cheese counter in Woolworth's, Dad suggests the same to her (you need to be sixteen to work for the Council). "I always have to do what Grace does," grumbles Susie. Nevertheless, since the aroma of cheese makes her quite ill, she writes off as I do and is eventually offered a Saturday job at Perry Common library, a beautiful art deco building dating from 1934. It is also on the No 7 bus route, in the area of Birmingham sometimes known as Little Ireland, so that's OK, and I feel smug because it is still on the Browne issue. I am technologically superior. This is what Harold calls the White Heat of Technology.

"There's a pub opposite," reports Susie, "and they sit in there singing Irish rebel songs. They say they've got IRA collecting boxes. Every so often, a bloke rushes over and asks us to photocopy the words to *The Lament for Robert Emmet*. He's really polite." Mom and Dad laugh. But once again, I feel a goose walk over my grave.

I stay on at Central Library until just before my A Levels, when I regretfully hand in my notice so as to have more study time.

8

Strikes and Strife,
Change and Conflict

1970–1974

When I look back at the Sixties, as a wistful teenager, it seems like a golden decade. The family were all together and there were no deaths, divorces or illnesses. My parents were shop stewards in a Birmingham full of buzzing employment – the Workshop of the World, the City of a Thousand and One Trades. We all danced to the music of the Beatles and Merseybeat, and led the world in fashions and hairstyles – I remember my aunts in miniskirts, Dusty Springfield bouffant bobs and Mary Quant geometric cuts, and my Mom with her beehive, dressed every Saturday at Margaret's of Six Ways, and stiff with lacquer. The Moon landing of 1969. And my parents, Labour Party members, were so pleased that Harold Wilson was in power, and his legislation. The Open University. The World Cup. Equal Pay for Women. Homosexuality legalised. The Race Relations Act of 1968. University grants. And Birmingham itself, still a Victorian city, its red brick beauty always glowing in what seemed to be perpetual golden sunlight.

Dad toasted in the New Year, 1st January 1970, "Here's to a great decade for us, Birmingham and Britain!" It isn't, of course. It begins with the Beatles disbanding in April 1970; it's the end of an era. The Soundtrack of the Sixties, that lost golden decade.

We all watch open mouthed and tense as the Apollo 13 drama is played out on live TV. The World Cup 1970 begins with great expectations, but is soiled by the Bobby Moore arrest. Bobby comes back fighting, backed by Sir Alf, and the England vs Brazil match is still one of the greatest I have ever seen, culminating in the famous swapping of shirts by Moore and Pele. But then England, after being 2-0 up, make a sad exit to West Germany in a 4-2 loss. "At least Brazil won it," mutters Dad. "Well there's always 1974."

But England do not even qualify in 1974 and Sir Alf, my dad's hero of the 1960s, is sacked. He's not the only hero Dad loses. Harold Wilson loses power in the 1970 General election on 18th June, despite the polls having predicted a confident Labour victory for months. "That's it," announced Dad, "I'm leaving the Labour Party." This is a posh way of saying he's not renewing his subscription; "I'm going to complete my OU course, and get into Management."

Although my parents cordially loathe Ted Heath ("The Unions will soon bring him down," predicts Dad), they are cheered by the 1973 entry into the EEC under Heath.

"Very good for trade and industry," says Dad.

"Very good for women, paid maternity leave," rejoins Mom.

Harold does make a comeback in February 1974, followed by a second vote in October, but by then Dad is foreman, working towards Management and has lost interest.

"Harold was the only PM who could work with the Unions. There's nothing wrong with asking for better pay and working conditions. But Harold's lost his spark."

Ted Heath is replaced by a woman called Margaret Thatcher. "I don't know how she'll work out," opines Mom. Her heroine was Barbara Castle. Harold, minus much of his enthusiasm, lasts till 1976, and is replaced by Jim Callaghan.

"I don't know how he'll turn out," mutters Dad.

Mom, for the first time ever, voted Liberal. "I liked Jeremy Thorpe," she explains, an opinion which later changes following his court case. Mom is disgusted, though not because of his homosexuality, which doesn't bother her at all.

"You don't shoot dogs in this country!"

It is, of course, a decade of death, divorce and illness for my family. I am a teenager, not a happy child. My body is changing, my face is changing. My sister is growing away from me. My teenage trials, the spots, oily hair, the puppy fat, the period pains, make me miserable. And the fashions of the 1970s are so ugly: the flared trousers, wedge-heeled shoes and boots, ponchos, sheepskin coats, midi skirts. My school uniform is ugly. My Littlewood's overall is ugly. And according to Mom and Dad, the music that Susie and I listen to on *Top of the Pops* is also ugly Glitter Rock.

And Birmingham is changing. The intentions are good. Herbert Manzoni, the City Engineer and Surveyor and architect John Madin intend to create a Birmingham fit for us to live and work in, and those of us who grew up in houses without central heating, hot running water and inside baths and toilets can appreciate that. We have a severe housing crisis. The rebuilding programme is known starkly as slum clearance; parts of *Cathy Come Home* were filmed in Birmingham. The women of Birmingham marched for better housing. This rebuilding has in fact been anticipated as far back as the war when thousands of homes were destroyed, and it included high density housing and tower blocks.

But the style of architecture they like Brutalist concrete can look pretty awful, and a great deal of old Birmingham goes under the bulldozer to make way for it. Streets, shops, libraries, cinemas, the Victorian Reference Library, Snow Hill Station, the Mason Science College and William Cowper School all meet the wrecker's ball. They make way for the Inner Ring Road, the Middle Ring Road, the Outer Ring Road, the Queensway, the Central Library, the Rotunda, Spaghetti Junction and Alpha Tower.

One or two bits are nice. Mom and Dad take us to the J F Kennedy Mosaic at St Chad's Circus, close to St Chad's Cathedral, which was also threatened with demolition. Less nice, we think, is the King Kong statue in the Manzoni Gardens. "The film was much better," says Mom, who saw it during the war at the Globe Cinema, and fled home in terror.

In 1971, Mom walks us up Summer Lane, to see the official opening of the Queensway, by the Queen. We see her from a distance, just her back, but Mom is thrilled. The Queensway has been planned since 1943, for a city where everyone can drive everywhere by car. But the 'Concrete Collar,' as it is known as, rapidly becomes unpopular with the council, as it prevents the city centre from expanding. Much worse for us pedestrians, it also involves the building of underpasses, which rapidly become no go areas which stink of urine.

It all seemed to go bad quite quickly.

And then there are the housing estates with their tower blocks. They do of course give us decent housing with our gardens, bathrooms, toilets, running hot water and central heating. But they are grey, ugly and concrete. Even the playgrounds, which we soon abandon, are ugly and concrete. The few flowers are scentless and thorny. The new park built for the estate next to Lucas's Great King Street is nothing but rather artificially green grass and is inhabited by some rather dubious characters. We soon abandon it for Tower Street, which has a playground and a parkie.

Dad tries out, with Uncle Albert, all the new pubs on the estate, the King of the Road, The Lamplighter, The Griffin and The Paddock, but soon abandons them with relief for the comforting Victorian surroundings of the Clements and the Bartons Arms.

A great deal goes on at St George's Church in the middle of the ersatz park, thanks to Mr Brown the vicar, but as Mom points out, it is a functional building which does not have the beauty of the demolished St George's in the Fields, where they got married.

I see signs of vandalism for the first time – graffiti, phone boxes which don't work and stink of urine, broken bottles, rubbish thrown on the street. The ugliness of our surroundings in fact mirrors the ugliness of the decade and my own personal and family trauma.

There are some changes which take some getting used to.

The coinage is decimalised in 1974. For those of us who grew up with pounds, shillings and pence, it is a huge change. We have special lessons at school; I struggle with them, thinking bitterly of the hours spent on pounds, shillings and pence at primary school. Mom and Dad buy both of us a little blue plastic wallet with the new coinage, but they don't have the beauty of our old silver shillings and sixpences, our copper threepenny bits and farthings.

Then there are the boundary changes. The Local Government Act of 1972 changes the face of the UK forever. The county of the West Midlands is created, but the significant difference for us is that Birmingham is no longer part of the County of Warwickshire. "Girls," says my headmistress, "always remember that you were born in the county of Warwickshire, as it is Shakespeare's county."

There are also massive changes in the Black Country and West Bromwich, but the big change for us is that the Royal Town of Sutton Coldfield is now part of Birmingham, which causes huge indignation in the friends and family members who live there. They join an organisation called SCOUT (Sutton Coldfield Out). However, for us, it means quite simply that we no longer have to pay to go into the park, formerly free only for those who lived in the area. We can also swim in the open air lido.

Grammar schools are being phased out slowly, since the Council voted to get rid of them in 1965, but not us: King Edward's has opted to be independent though not fee paying, but now highly selective. There are a few others like this: all the King Edward's schools, Bishop Vesey, Handsworth

Grammar and some of the Catholic schools. It is a running battle. A 1973 petition to save King Edward's is launched, and there is a rally in the city centre. "Well, they're already in," says Dad, "but it wasn't a fair system. Picking kids at the age of eleven." He falls silent, remembering how he as an orphan in 1939, had to turn down his Grammar School place at King Edward's Aston, because his family were too poor to send him. That's why we're there instead. He rewrote the past. "It's hard on some kids," says Mom, "Poor David Burke, so clever, failed because the exam made him sick with nerves."

Then there are the strikes. I've always been aware of industrial things; my parents are both shop stewards. As he works in the day and she works evenings, they have always openly discussed their cases over the dinner table, where they see each other. Dad's big thing is Health and Safety; Mom's is equal pay for women. "And," she adds, "some kind of system where women are paid when off work when pregnant, and their jobs are kept open for them." She lost her job twice when pregnant, and she made lampshades at home for Mr Wallace Lawler (another sad loss at the beginning of the decade – Mr Lawler died of a massive heart attack in 1972). "Living in fantasy land there, Lil," says Dad, "but might come with this Common Market thing."

Dad's theory was that Harold worked with the unions, and that the Unions will soon bring Ted Heath down. Then there is one strike after another. In the late 1960s, government and Unions did begin to grow apart, and 1970 begins with a bang with a series of strikes. The Colour Strike in 1970 by ITV technicians is because they refuse to work with colour technology without a pay rise. This doesn't interest us, although we have an ATV studio in Aston, because we still have a black and white TV.

There are some strikes particular to the West Midlands. 1972 sees workers at the West Midlands Gas Board voting to strike, and we see them assemble outside the Gas Works in Saltley. Dunlop workers at the Dunlop Factory also vote to go on strike for equal pay with other Midlands car workers in May 1970. And in 1979, a bus driver industrial dispute means a late departure for some holidaymakers from Digbeth Bus Station.

Then 1971 sees the very first ever postal workers strike and 1972 brings a builders' strike, and the big one in 1972: the Miners' Strike. We take some notice of this because it culminates in the Battle of Saltley Gate in 1972, when 2,000 NUM pickets descend on a coke works in Birmingham and are joined by thousands of workers from across the city. Then so many local strikes: the Ford workers in Dagenham in 1971, the Thames dock strike in 1972, Tate & Lyle in 1974, the Rail strike of 1970, Rolls Royce in 1971, Kodak in 1973, the sit in strike of Manchester in 1972, the tanker drivers' strike (meaning a shortage of oil), the Traffic Signallers' Strike in London in 1970... the list goes on and on, millions of days lost, discontented workers, disruption and chaos. A nation polarised.

Even my Dad has had his little experience. The day workers at Tucker's come in one morning and find a cricket bat on one of the benches; clearly the night shift have been having fun. One of the managers orders the men to remove it; it is not their job, they say. They are going to walk out. Dad and Johnnie Murray are summoned to sort out this volatile situation. "Faults on both sides," remarks Dad mildly, after on the spot mediation, "Unions and Management not talking. In Germany and Japan, they're talking and hammering out sensible working and pay agreements. If we're not careful, in a generation, they'll be leading the world in trade and manufacturing."

In the meantime, the Heath government has passed the Industrial Relations Act of 1971, making the closed shop illegal, compulsory ballots before strikes, and setting up Industrial Relations Courts to judge where unions are said to have broken agreements. "All suggested by Barbara Castle in her 1968 paper *In Place of Strife*," remarks my Mom, ever faithful to her heroine.

Susie and I are really only interested if it affects us. There is a wave of teachers' strikes in 1973 and we are hopeful that school might close down, but sadly it turns out that only a few of the teachers are union members, and they tend to be the younger and trendier ones who teach our favourite subjects. They seem rather embarrassed about being on strike and it is all very polite.

Then, in 1974, comes the Bread Strike. In December 1974, the bakers of Britain decide to switch off their ovens and demand a 66% pay rise; they want £30 for a 40 hour week, the end of Sunday working, and an extra week's holiday. At school, Mrs Garrett offers lunchtime baking sessions, but Mom is not able to find the flour and yeast we need. So we make some rather curious flat bread but Dad chips his tooth on it and says he'd rather have crackers; unfortunately, these are also in short supply.

At the weekend, Mom is fed up with a week's queuing, and says to Susie and me, "Go out and don't come back without some bread." Sighing, we put on coats, hats, scarves and gloves and drift out of the house. We part by mutual consent, she wandering off to the Newtown Precinct, where there are a couple of bakeries, Wimbush's and The Crumb (no chance at the supermarkets – you have to go somewhere where they are baking on site). I wander off down Summer Lane, towards Ye Olde Newtown Bakery.

I would say that when I reach Ye Olde Bakery I am aghast, but I don't reach Ye Olde Bakery, I reach the end of the queue for Ye Olde Bakery. Ye Olde Bakery is baking bread and the average waiting time is three hours, at the end of which, frozen to the bone, I receive a ration of one loaf and six cobs, the same as Susie gets. We are very glad when this is all over. "I don't know why people get nostalgic about rationing and queuing during the war," grumbles Susie. "Two women were fighting over the last packet of yeast in Sainsbury's," says Mom.

The famous Longbridge plant in Northfield is crippled by strikes in the 1970s. Longbridge has been there since Herbert Austin founded the Austin Motor Company in 1905. In 1975, it is nationalised as British Leyland. Mom and Dad read in the *Birmingham Evening Mail* of the exploits of Red Robbo, who is said to be responsible for 523 strikes alone. "There's no doubt the quality of our cars has gone down," sighs Dad, "but you can't blame workers wanting decent pay and working conditions."

All this culminates in the Three Day Week of 1974.

Throughout the 1970s, wages have been capped to cope with inflation. We ourselves have been worse off, as have many of our friends, who have to pretend their phones are out of order when they cannot pay the phone bill and get cut off. Wages simply do not cover the cost of living.

Dad works a forty hour week and does a pools round on Friday nights. Mom works at Lucas's afternoons (she is now line supervisor) and runs a *Burlington* catalogue. Yet we too never have enough money; life is more expensive than in Guildford Street. The rent is more, the gas and electricity are more now that we have central heating instead of a weekly delivery of coal. They need to find our bus fare, school meals and uniform money.

Then there is the Hire Purchase on the new washing machine, the Music Centre, the telly, and the purchase of things we never used to have but now everyone takes for granted. Things like hair dryers or fridges.

Dad does all the painting and decorating in the house himself, all the gardening, and spends every Saturday stretched out under the ever faulty A60. He cannot afford a new car. Mom has stopped going to Margaret's of Six Ways and colours and curls her hair herself. They do not of course have credit cards or overdraft facilities. Nobody does.

Susie and I practise our own small economies like getting off the bus on Great Hampton Street and walking through the estate to save a second bus fare from Birmingham. Assuring our parents we would rather take in sandwiches than have school dinners (this is true), not asking for piano and violin lessons, and not telling them about the school trips. "Our lives are getting worse, not better," grumbles Mom, and this is quite simply because they haven't had a decent pay rise in years.

Then we have the Three Day week.

This is to do with militant action by the National Union of Mineworkers (NUM). They want a pay rise and have implemented an overtime ban short of a strike, and as most of our power stations are coal fuelled, this means shortages. To conserve stocks and cut electricity consumption, Ted Heath announces on 13th December 1973 the Three Day Week, to come into force on 31st December. The NUM strike does not actually start until 5th February, by which time, we have suffered a month of the Three Day Week.

On the 9th January, the miners walk out, after rejecting a pay offer.

What affects everybody most is the telly going off at 10.30pm, but not Susie and I, as we are already in bed by then after watching the earlier exciting TV coverage of pickets. Mom and Dad shrug, then put Radio Two on (batteries) and light the candles. All commercial users of electricity are prohibited to three days of electricity and no overtime, though the essential services are exempt.

Then we suffer power cuts, when a state of emergency is declared on 9th February. Some places can suffer up to nine hours without electricity. At Lucas's, Mom sits at her machine with a blanket around her. Dad walks round Tucker's in his winter coat, carrying a torch. At school, huge cheers go up if we have a power cut. But King Edward's *never* closes; we sit in our coats, scarves and gloves while wild rumours sweep the school that the ink has frozen in the inkwells.

Many industries lay their staff off, and it is said that the number of unemployed has doubled. Some of those who are down to three days are able to claim the Dole. When we seem to be at a stalemate, Ted Heath calls a snap election and seems terribly surprised to lose it. Labour form a minority government, immediately increase miners' wages by 35%, which the miners accept by 25th February, and by 7th March, this rather exciting time is all over.

Dad is ecstatic to see Labour and Harold back in power. "The Tories won't forget though," he says. "They'll always remember that the miners held the country to ransom. Heath's gone, but somebody will come along there who'll try to smash the Unions for good. And Labour also made a rod for their own backs."

The Winter of Discontent is still some way off. As is Margaret Thatcher.

9

Tearing the Heart
out of Birmingham

1974

Thursday 21st November 1974 is a Thursday like any other. It is of course pay day in Brum. I have been to the Youth Club in the evening, while Susie watched *Top of the Pops* and then *Mastermind*. At eight o'clock, we are sitting in our dressing gowns, pink and blue, in front of the telly bracing ourselves for going up to bed.

At eight seventeen, we hear a distant thumping or banging noise. We are used to this – we live close to Spaghetti Junction and the motorway – so we take no notice.

Then, at eight twenty-seven, we hear another, louder bang. This time Dad goes outside and looks around, looking for an accident. He looks to the left, where the motorway and Spaghetti Junction are. "I think it came from the direction of town," says Mom dubiously.

It is not until the Nine o'clock News comes on that we find ourselves looking in shock at the terrible, terrible footage of the aftermath of the Birmingham Bombings.

This was the most difficult chapter to write of this book. I spoke to people who still cried at the recollection of it. This chapter is not an account of the Troubles, the Bombings, or the Birmingham Six – rivers of ink have flowed on those subjects. Instead, it is a personal account of how the Bombings affected our family, friends and city.

Susie and I are sent off to bed as Mom and Dad think the news is too dreadful for us. And even as we sleep, the city is in chaos. *The Mulberry Bush* and *The Tavern in the Town* are smoking heaps. Twenty-one are dead, or will die, and two hundred and twenty are injured, some with life changing injuries – such as loss of limbs and sight. A firefighter entering one of the pubs sees a shrieking, limbless torso. There is a smell of burnt flesh. All bus services into the city centre are halted and my cousins, who are there, have to walk home. All the major roads into the City Centre are closed. Taxi drivers are being asked to ferry the wounded to hospital and those with Irish accents are often attacked. A temporary treatment centre has been set up as the hospitals are full. Irish nurses, including my mom's friend Philomena Griffin, are also sworn and spat at. A cousin of mine is sitting in the Odeon and it rocks from side to side, twice. The manager comes out and asks them to sit still. Eventually, he manages to get out and because the buses are no longer running, walks home, getting there at three in the morning. New Street is the heart of the city and the heart has been ripped out.

The Troubles have in fact been part of my life as far back as I can remember and we live in a city with one of the UK's largest Irish populations; much of the workforce is Irish, most of Mom and Dad's friends are Irish, and our auntie is Irish.

When I get up the next day, Dad has already left for work. Mom is in the kitchen looking at the *Daily Mirror* headlines and shaking her head, but she says nothing. Susie and I eat our breakfast in silence. We have recently started travelling to school separately, meeting various friends en route, but Mom says suddenly, "I want you to travel there and back together, today." Our eyes meet across the table.

As we get ready to go out, she comes over and ties our navy blue headscarves under our chins, and buttons up our coats. This is unusual. I think she thinks she is sending us out into an unknown world. Last night, many people sent out their children for the last time. She says, carefully, trying not to frighten us, "I don't want you to catch the bus into Birmingham today. I want you to get on the 5 or 7 at Summer Lane and get off at the bottom, opposite Yardley's, and cross over there for the 70. I want you to come back that way, or get off at the Pelican Works if you like, and I'll look out the window for both of you." She stands at the door and waves us off; she stands looking till we are out of view.

The atmosphere on the bus is very subdued, with many people gazing in horror at the newspaper. Before the Internet, before 24 hour news channels, the newspapers and the radio were how we picked the news up. The top of the bus is thick with cigarette smoke. The raindrops running down the windows are like tears.

Our bus route means we avoid the centre of town, as Mom intended and when we get to school, we head off for our classrooms, for Registry and then Assembly. At this point we usually separate; the Catholic girls who are mainly Irish though some are Poles, go to separate classrooms where, much to our envy, they colour in pictures of the Virgin Mary and clutch their rosaries. This all seems very glamorous to us and moreover, they are not down on their knees. However, as the register is being taken, one of the prefects pops her head around the door, "Miss Sargeant says can all girls please go into Hall first."

We look upon each other with a wild surmise. The Door Monitor opens the door for Mrs Davies (English, young, trendy, short skirts, floating hair) and we march into Hall. Miss Sargeant, small, plump, brisk and also Scottish, looks like a robin in her red dress and black robes; she has replaced tall, thin austere Miss Reid, who went back to the private sector. When seated on the Throne, the tiny Miss Sargeant uses a footstool.

Miss Sargeant stands before us on the platform. "Girls, I know it is usual for Protestants and Catholics, indeed all faiths, to separate for Prayers and reunite for Assembly. However, just for once, just for today, I am asking that we all unite for Prayer and pray for Birmingham. Any girl who is not comfortable with this may leave now."

Our heads turn. Nobody moves. With a great clattering of chairs, we sink to our knees and pray for our devastated city.

That night over tea, Mom and Dad discuss their day. The *Birmingham Evening Mail* is full of it; Susie and I gaze at the scenes of devastation. "The atmosphere was terrible at Tucker's," says Dad, subdued. "Then Johnnie Murray came in and rushed up to me. He said over and over, it wasn't us Bill, it wasn't the ordinary Irish. We shook hands in front of all the men. This calmed things down a bit."

This is not Bert's story when he comes in to do the pools with Dad. Bert has worked at Longbridge since he was fourteen, apart from the six years he was in the RAF. Bert has seen everything. "They chased the Irish out of Longbridge today," he says to Dad. "Men I've worked with for years. They said they were going to hang them. Said they'd go on strike if the Irish weren't kicked out." Bert pauses to light a Woodbine. His mild face is puzzled. "I was with the Irish in the RAF," he says. "Not their fight, but they joined it."

Mom shakes her head.

News at Ten tells us the police are looking for the perpetrators; that a third bomb was destroyed in a controlled explosion on the Hagley Road. That two of the dead were two Irish brothers, Desmond and Eugene Reilly. That some of the victims have lost arms and legs. That somebody has been blinded by shrapnel. That somebody else was deafened. That most of the dead were aged between 17 and 30. That reprisals are feared by loyalists in Northern Ireland and that there have been attacks on Irish businesses, pubs and shops.

Saturday morning brings huge dilemmas for Dad. Throughout all this, Birmingham has continued to function as far as it can with a paralysed city centre. Therefore, I am at work as usual at Central Library on Saturday at the very top of New Street, and Susie is off to Perry Common Library, in the heart of Birmingham IRA country. As for Mom, she remarks that after her usual battle with the twin tub and her Carmen electric rollers, she is off to town and the Bull Ring as usual, and the IRA won't stop her.

Now all three of his womenfolk are heading into danger and Dad doesn't know what to do. He eventually works out a very complicated escort itinerary and this involves him dropping me off at Central using a very convoluted route while Susie catches the No 7 bus to Perry Common with many a warning about suspicious packages.

When I arrive at Central Library, we enter not via the main doors, but a side door where the caretakers are waiting. Usually they let us in without even looking at our staff badges. But today is different. The caretakers are standing behind two hastily pushed together tables. I hear a phrase I have never heard before and will hear for the next twenty years, "Check your bags, please!"

"But we're the staff," says someone, bewildered.

The caretakers cannot meet our eyes. "From now on, we will check the bags of everyone entering this building."

This means the public as well, but it's an oblique way of saying that many of the staff are Irish and are under suspicion. After all, we don't know who the bombers are. Standing in front of me is somebody I'll call Brian Flynne. Brian is a junior librarian; he is second generation Irish, born in Birmingham of first generation Irish and like so many, his accent is a hybrid of Brummie and Irish. He is very good looking, with dark hair and blue eyes, and I admire him vainly from afar. Brian is openly pro a united Ireland – so are many people, including my parents – and he is open in his support of the IRA. He goes around Central Library expressing his support and we just shrug. Why? Because it's Brian, he's a colleague. Because he's a Brummie, just like us. *Because we never thought it would happen.*

As the caretakers speak and check, Brian turns round, unable to meet them eye to eye. I see his face. I look into Hell. *It wasn't me. I thought I could say what I liked, but I never thought this would happen. It was my fault, too. I enabled it.*

Joan puts me on the counter in the morning. It is, in fact, quite busy. Every library in Birmingham is open and was open yesterday. At ten o'clock, the phone rings; it is Susie, calling from Perry Common. I am oddly glad to know she got there safely.

She says, "Are you a lert?"

"A lert?" I ask doubtfully. "What is a lert?"

"No, no, don't be daft. ALERT, are you alert. There's a memo went round on the van yesterday, we all have to be ALERT. You need to read it."

I look around and can't see anything, but I say I will go and look for it.

Her voice drops, "There's a rumour going round here..."

She mentions a name, in a whisper. "They say he's a bomber. But I know him. He's not a killer."

Soon, the names of the Birmingham Six will be known around the world. But already there are rumours. And doubts.

After she hangs up, I go off into the staff work room next to the counter, and find indeed a hastily typed memo dated 22nd November 1974. It occurs to me that when it was typed, Xeroxed and sent out, all the libraries must have been open as usual. I think of something Mom says, "Oh, if we were bombed in Lozells overnight during the war, I used to get up and go to work in the Jewellery Quarter the day after as usual. Put my tin hat on."

I take it back to the counter and read it. It says indeed that we are to be Alert. That all bags coming into any library will be checked. That we must keep a lookout for suspicious packages, that we must open them and put our hands in and have a look. My eyes widen. I look up and see Joan looking at me. "Joan, I am not going to put my hand inside a suspicious package!"

The daughter of the shop stewards has spoken. There is a hastily arranged senior staff meeting and it is agreed that if we see suspicious packages, we will call Security. As the library is mainly occupied by students with bags, they are going to be very busy.

At lunch time, I take the lift up to a rather subdued staff canteen and eat my sandwiches. I don't really have mates here as I did at Littlewood's; I am the only Saturday assistant and I am by far the youngest of the staff. So I put on my coat and go and stand at the entrance to the library and stare down New Street. I can just see some barriers and rubble, and police moving around.

I am thinking about my coat. It is brown suedette, with a sheepskin collar, and came from C&A and my shoes, which are white, with platform soles and came from Dolcis. I am thinking about them because they are new and they are the kind of things I would wear for a night on the town, on pay day, on a Thursday night in Birmingham. You see, I am seventeen years old, exactly the same age as Jane Davis, who was killed in the blast. Jane will never wear her best coat and shoes again and I am now sixty-five; I have had the life Jane Davis was never allowed to live.

As, hands in pockets, I stare down New Street, I see Brian Flynne coming up. He is wearing a black overcoat and his head is down. As he stumbles up the steps, I move aside, but he comes right up to me and looks up. I flinch and rock back slightly on my platform heels. I said earlier that looking into his face was like looking into Hell. Well, in the course of the morning, Brian Flynne has passed through all nine circles of Dante's Hell, and is now bang in the middle. His eyes are burning black. He grabs my arm.

"Have you been there?"

I shake my head.

"Don't go there. Don't look. I've been there, I know what it's like," he whispers.

You had to be there. You had to see it. You had to know what it was like.

The afternoon is taken up with a drill, hastily arranged by Security. Everything is hastily arranged. We never expected it to happen. We weren't ready. We don't know what to do.

When the fire alarms go off, we all troop off into Victoria Square and hang around while the registers are taken, and Security do a mock search of the building. This is something we get very used to over the remaining year I am at the library; not just security drills but all those idiots who think it is fun to ring the library and say there is a bomb in the building. Out we all troop, Saturday after Saturday, into Victoria Square, greeting the Town Hall and Art Gallery and Museum staff who are going through the same procedure. We make many friends in this way. We learn to have our coats and bags with us at the counter so we don't have to go out into the cold without them. We get so blasé that we hang around in the hope that the search will take till 5pm, so we can all go home.

But we always do go out. Because you never know. We don't know that the IRA has now deemed Birmingham a no go area, because of the backlash. We will walk around like this for the next twenty-five years. Having your bag checked.

At five o'clock, I put on my coat, pick up my bag and take the elevator down to the main doors. As agreed, Mom and Dad are standing there. Dad has already picked up Susie, who finishes a bit earlier. Mom's face is like thunder as she puffs on her Peter Stuyvesant fag; normally she stays in town till six o'clock; another strike against the IRA. As for me, Dad has made a phone call to Stan Atkins. I was meeting Lynne Atkins tonight at the Birmingham Odeon for a film and he has cancelled it. I am touchingly pleased to see them and set off to go down New Street to the No 33 bus stop. But Dad catches my arm. "Not that way. This way," he says, gesturing down Colmore Row.

I am surprised, but we set off for the No 7 stop at Snow Hill. Years later, he says, "I got off the bus near New Street. I saw it. I was there. I didn't want you to see it and remember it like that." He buys a *Birmingham Evening Mail* from the man at his stand, yelling "Get your *Evening Mail!*" and glances at the latest bombing news.

We bump home down Summer Lane. Mom and Dad are behind me and I am squashed next to a man who is very drunk. He is regaling the No 7 with his exploits. He stinks of alcohol and his voice is slurred, "So I wen' in the Irish shop an' I knocked everyfink to the floor. An' I sez to them at the counter, I sez, that's for all the babs and they doan say a word." I glance behind. Mom and Dad are shaking their heads. But they say nothing. What can you say?

The backlash rolls on over the next few weeks. Our Irish auntie, Mom and Dad's Irish friends, all have to get used to abuse every time they open their mouths. And then there are the arrests. The trials. And life in a city under siege, where everywhere you go your bag is checked. And you don't know whether or not it might happen again. Even school is called out one afternoon, following a warning telephone call. We line up in the playground. "The boys from Handsworth Grammar, larking around," mutter the teachers.

The funerals.

Two of the victims were Irish, the brothers Desmond and Eugene Reilly. This is what happens when you bomb a city with one of the highest Irish populations in Britain. When I walk into the living room one night shortly after, Mom is sitting on the sofa, staring at the screen. An unseen announcer is interviewing Bridget Reilly, the mother of the two brothers. His voice is kind and low, but Bridget Reilly can hardly speak. Suddenly, he asks, "Is there anything at all that could make you feel better about this?"

Bridget Reilly breaks down at last into a storm of weeping, "No, nothing at all, never, nothing!"

Mom's face is frozen. Shortly after, she finds pictures of Bridget in the paper, which she shows to Dad – Bridget leading a walk for peace, Bridget at the funeral. We can see that Bridget is being propped up; she can hardly walk.

The sad catalogue of events rolls on. Bridget Reilly is refused service in shops. Staff in factories across the Midlands go on strike in protest. The terrible backlash against the Irish community. Retaliation attacks in Northern Ireland. The Prevention of Terrorism Act 1974. The Birmingham Six. The cancellation of our St Patrick's Day Parade, the third biggest in the world. The books, the documentaries, the films. The inquests. The rumours. Tensions that will last a generation. The two bangs that I can hear in my head to this very day. I didn't see it, thanks to the combined efforts of Mom and Dad and Brian Flynne. I wasn't there. But I heard it.

No closure, then or now, for any of us. It is our everlasting, eternal sorrow.

Were you there?

Where were you?

What were you doing?

Did you see it?

Did you hear it?

Did you know anyone who ...?

The questions Brummies of a certain age ask themselves, in place of the questions that were never answered.

In January 1975, I have an interview at Aberystwyth University, for a joint degree in English and Librarianship. This involves an epic three train journey in both directions, done in a day. I am wearing the serious, studious clothes I have bought specially for University interviews from Richard Shops: a long-sleeved white blouse, with a pointed collar and a blue pinafore dress, and my brand new winter pink woollen coat over them. The two lecturers who interview me are very pleasant; there are questions about my Saturday job in the library, the books I am reading. Then right at the end, they look at each other, and one leans forward and says gently, "I was just wondering. What was it like in Birmingham, when you were bombed?"

I sit and stare at them, speechless. So much I could say. The two bangs. A city centre paralysed. A community polarised. Bridget Reilly. The twenty-one. The 220 injured. Check your bags, please. The Birmingham Six. Walking around never knowing if it might happen again, if it might be you. The bomb scares at the library. The bomb scares at school. Eyeing up any suspicious package you see. Brian Flynne. Because next time, it's you.

Instead, I open my mouth, and stammer, "You had to be there. You had to know what it was like. You had to have seen it. You had to have heard it. I am seventeen. She – Jane Davis – was seventeen also. I am here, in my new clothes. She will never dress up and go anywhere ever again. It could have been me. I am soon eighteen. Maxine Hambleton was eighteen. We all went to the pubs from the age of seventeen and we drank a Britvic orange and played the jukebox, because they never asked. I have been given a life that was taken away from them. They could have gone to University. They could have done, or been, anything. And in Wales, you had Aberfan, I was nine, the same age as some of the victims. I had a life that was taken away from them. And my Mom and Dad said, maybe we'll get some decent health and safety because of Aberfan and maybe the Birmingham Bombings will lead to us all standing up and saying there should be peace in Northern Ireland. But all this should happen anyway, and all those innocent people shouldn't have died for it. And from where I'm sitting, it just all looks so pointless, as though they all died in vain."

In the ensuing silence, I remember something the Reverend Geoffrey Brown used to say and quote it: "In the midst of life, we are in death."

At which, they say no more.

I remember, when I was a little girl, Mom used to say, "We're a race apart, those of us who went through the war. You have to know what it was like, you have to have been there, the bombs dropped on your home and the factory where you worked. And I remember the night I stood out in the backyard looking up at the planes, and the sky was blood red. That was the bombing of Coventry."

In the same way, all of us whose cities and towns were subject to a terrorist attack are a race apart. Us. Belfast. Derry. Aldershot. London. Dublin. Guildford. Manchester. Warrington. Omagh. So many others. A list of sorrow. A catalogue of tragedy, British and Irish. You have to know what it was like. You have to have been there. You had to see it. You had to tell yourself that they died so there might be peace, because you had to make sense out of the senseless.

*   *   *

After I finished writing this chapter, I went and looked at the two memorials to the victims of the Birmingham Bombings. The stone at St Philip's Cathedral, with all the names inscribed on a plaque, recently visited by Michael Higgins, president of all Ireland. And then the three steel trees at New Street Station, every leaf bearing the name of a victim, paid for by the Birmingham Irish Association. I sat out in the gentle autumn sun. I felt some peace.

In Memoriam, the twenty-one dead and the two hundred and twenty who suffered often life changing injuries. When, on one terrible night, the heart was torn out of our city.

IO

Senior School

1971–1973

In 1971, I enter the GCE stream at school for the two years leading up to my O Levels. I have, of course, made all the completely wrong choices for study. For a start, school looks down its nose at CSEs, and I should really be doing Maths CSE. Picking the sciences was also a mistake; I should have done the much easier General Science. Latin is simply because Dad can't face the thought of Mom confronting genial Herr Mayer on Parents' Night. Anything enjoyable, such as Cookery, Needlework, Art or Pottery is stuck in a column with something supposed to be essential. PE, Dance and Games, are to our general disgust, still compulsory, as we regard ourselves as too old and sophisticated for them.

This is something of a puzzle to me, as the girls in all my library books are mad about games. It seems to matter if you win a hockey match or not. Whereas we just really don't care. "Girls," exhorts the head of Hanover House during a termly House meeting, "please get down to the courts today to support Hanover House in the Inter House Netball Tournament." Which we dutifully, and uninterestedly, do. I don't like netball as I am so small and the taller girls bounce the ball on my head. And I really don't care if Hanover House wins the School Trophy or not. This is not Angela Brazil.

Once a week, we are still transported on a Corporation bus to the school playing grounds, where we change into our Aertex blouses and skirts. This is all right in the summer for rounders and athletics, but is foul in the winter, when we pound up and down the hockey field. "It's not cold," exhort Mrs Craddock and Miss Mold, the Games mistresses. "It's all right for them," mutters Lesley, "they've got track suits on."

Already susceptible to colds, I now catch a permanent one. Mom is galvanized into action. She gets the ever helpful Dr Carolan to write a letter to school saying that I am too frail for winter games. This means I join the contingent of sickly girls who still have to traipse off to the playing fields on the weekly Corporation bus, but go for walks round the field instead, which means you get to keep your coat, hat, gloves and scarf on.

Susie is not as fortunate as me. She is good at hockey, against her will; this is what I longed for when I read my boarding school books, the council estate girl coming good and scoring the last minute winner for St Sharon's against the rivals, as the other girls cheer her hoarse. She doesn't care (as the rest of us don't), but she is chosen to be in the junior school hockey team and she has to be in Inter School and County matches. These take place on Saturday mornings, and she and Dad moan and groan as they get up early and take off in the A60 to a muddy, windswept field somewhere in Warwickshire.

Dad returns from his first girls' hockey match in trauma. "Never seen anything like it," he says to Mom, as he lights a cigarette with a shaking hand. "I've never seen violence like that even in the Forces, or at the Boxing Club. When they bully off, they don't go for the ball, they go for the other girl's legs, and those hockey sticks are used as *weapons*. Us dads were wincing on the side; never expected to see Susie come out of it alive. Some of the blokes had to go for a drink straight after. Female of the species, especially with a weapon in their hands." As Susie is covered with bruises, and mud which clogs up the twin tub, Mom decides that Susie is also delicate and prone to colds and the ever obliging Dr Carolan provides the usual letter. Susie returns with relief to *Tiswas*, and Dad to *Grandstand*.

Music seems to have died a natural death unless you are doing it for O Level ("Thank God I don't have to listen to them playing the recorder anymore," says Dad sincerely), but we do gather in the Hall once a week for singing with the hapless Mr Billington, wincing as we trill *Nymphs and Shepherds*.

One sign of our new maturity and status as top of the lower school, Lower and Upper Fifth, is that we are allowed to remove the bibs from our school skirts. This is, of course, to accommodate our growing busts. Apart from that, there are no other concessions to our teen sensibilities. Our hair is still tied neatly back, our shoes are flat and our skirts on the knee. Some of the girls roll the waist over as soon as they get out of school, in the vain hope of attracting the Handsworth Grammar lads, but of course, this just gives you a lumpy waist. Makeup and hair colouring is strictly forbidden. We read the *Jackie* under the cover of the desktop. At breaktime, we discuss *Pick of the Pops* on Sunday, and T. Rex's latest single. Fridays are given over to discussion of *Top of the Pops*, though the more intellectual girls prefer to discuss the BBC's production of *War and Peace*. The girls debate the merits of the Osmonds versus the Jackson Five. We have all grown out of *Magpie, Skippy, Daktari* and *Look In*.

School is also involved in various charitable enterprises. Our School charity is the sponsorship of Bimola, a little girl in Biafra, and the monies we raise are intended to help Bimola become a teacher, and return to teach in the village she comes from. We have regular updates from Bimola in the form of letters she writes to us, read out at Assembly.

The school year rolls around as it has always done: back to school in September, Speech Day, the Christmas Carols concert, the Spring Fair, the Flower Show, House Meetings, the inter school and inter county and city sports tournaments, Sports Day, plays and concerts with the School Orchestra and the School Choir. And the school day is unchanged: register, assembly and prayers, lessons, break with milk and iced buns, dinner, lunchtime clubs (I'm in Debating and Drama), volunteer work in the library and home time. Once a year, we have the paperback Book Fair in the library, where I show my sophistication by purchasing *Tess of the D'Urbervilles* and *Richard the Third* instead of *The Chalet School Does It Again*.

Z Class now splits up though for lessons, our O Level choices and our Divisions. Divisions, applicable only to English Language and Maths, are King Edward's only admission that maybe not everybody is as good at a subject as they might be. They look down their noses at the CSE qualification: we are all to do O Levels. I am in the top division for English, but I soon slide to the lowest Division for Maths; despite poor Miss Naish's best efforts, we have already decided that we are failures. I spend the lessons writing stories in my rough book, the notebook we have all been issued with.

English Language and English Literature are with Mrs Davies, who is young and trendy like most of the English teachers, and who wears floaty scarves around her neck. She is also form mistress and gives me reading lists to take to the library. We have O Level set texts: Thomas Hardy's *The Mayor of Casterbridge, Macbeth* and a compilation of Modern Poetry. We point out to Mrs Davis that none of these poets are female, and she agrees mournfully.

Reading *The Mayor of Casterbridge* gets me interested in the BBC costume dramas of the 70s, and they do indeed show it, with Alan Bates as the Mayor and Robert Powell, who many of the girls fancy in *Doomwatch*, as Jude the Obscure. These are not in fact very cheerful and I prefer David Rintoul in *Pride and Prejudice*.

French is with Miss Allen, a cheerful Northerner, who tells us exciting stories of when she was in Paris during the student riots of 1968. As well as language, we are studying *Jean Valjean*, an extract from *Les Miserables*, which we consider very dull.

Religious Studies, formerly known as Scripture, is taken by Mr Dolman. Tall and thin, he has glasses and frizzy hair, and addresses me as Miss Holte. This was chosen in preference to Geography, but in fact we rather enjoy the discussions on subjects such as abortion and the study of world faiths, especially the visit of a kindly Sikh from Handsworth who tells us all about his faith. The set texts are books from the New Testament, and we develop a cordial dislike of St Paul and his views on women.

Rather to our surprise, Mr Dolman and Miss Allen have a Romance, something of a novelty in a school that frowns upon such things. The romance is mainly expressed by their meeting outside the school gates at 4pm and walking to the bus stop together, while the rest of us goggle. Their marriage also causes a sensation in the school, and many of us turn up at the wedding to see them leave the church, forming a schoolgirl guard of honour. Shortly after O Level year, Mr Dolman leaves to enter the Methodist ministry, possibly, in our view due to the embarrassment of being one of the few married men in a school of Misses and moreover, being married to one of the teachers there. But more likely due to a vocation. His predecessor, gentle Mr Arnold, left to be a missionary.

I am one of the few girls doing Latin, with Miss Boggis, Deputy Head Mistress and an excellent teacher, a disciplinarian who loves her subject. We struggle with the grammar and the 300 dull lines of Virgil's *Aeneid*, which is the set text. Miss Boggis occasionally unbends enough to tell us about her days in the WRENS in the war, including, to our fascinated horror, Lord Nuffield's generous donation of free sanitary towels to the WRENS. This is the kind of thing That Is Not Mentioned (but is still interesting).

History is still with Mrs Thorne. We have slogged through history from the Stone Age to the nuclear age, and what we've had to do included the Hundred Years War, the Civil War, the Thirty Years War and the Seven Years War etc. Now, maybe, it might be time to do something more interesting; how did we get through the entire reign of Henry the Eighth without mention of the Six Wives? But to our dismay, the syllabus is all about Whigs and Tories, political reform Acts and the Corn Laws. We even do the French Revolution and the Napoleonic Wars without one mention of Josephine and the Scarlet Pimpernel. "Will we ever," we ask her, "do any history that might just be about women – or girls like us, whose parents work in factories?" Mrs Thorne shrugs, and reminds us of the Industrial Revolution. "But that's all about people who made money out of it, not us, who made the money for them," we mutter.

I triumphantly reference *A Christmas Carol*, the figures of Ignorance and Want, based on Dickens' reading of the Factory Inspectors Acts, in which it was pointed out that children in Birmingham were beginning work at the age of eight, working from two in the morning till six at night. In order to avert rebellion, although she is actually quite sympathetic, Mrs Thorne tells us she is working on a history of the School, which will by default have females in it.

But by far the worst is Science.

For some reason, possibly seduced by the glamour of the Science labs and the bottle green or navy blue Science overall, I elected to do Physics, Chemistry and Biology, instead of General Science, the easier option. This was a big mistake. I am completely out of my depth. All these subjects are a mystery and they are not fun; there is no more messing around with Bunsen burners and test tubes. Chemistry, with the fierce Mr Clark, is all about chemical equations. Physics is with Mr Hutchinson, a man in his eighties, who is equally fierce and he tells us it is a waste of time educating girls. "Why are you here, then?" we mumble.

Mrs Eagleton and Mrs Wragge, who teach Biology, are more sympathetic, but the subject has also become a mystery to me. We are allowed to drop subjects before O Level following the twice yearly Christmas and summer exams, and after I score all time lows in the three Sciences, I am, with relief, allowed to drop them and devote myself to the Humanities.

Home life is very different now. In fact, we are not so badly off since Dad got promoted to foreman, Mom went back to work, and Susie and I got Saturday jobs. The house has been carpeted and we have a mustard coloured Post Office telephone. Susie and I have hair dryers, transistor radios to listen to Radios Luxembourg and Caroline, and a tape recorder to record the plays I write and which we perform with Kim Harrison. We have enough Saturday job money to buy singles by T. Rex, and dance to them on Mom and Dad's brand new Music Centre.

Susie and I no longer dress alike in clothes from the Co-op. We cannot persuade Mom to set foot in Chelsea Girl, and Miss Selfridge and Richard

Shops are too expensive, but she does unbend enough to take us to Gear Cellar in C&A, where we choose clothes that are really rather dreadful, although nothing can ever match the horror of our platform boots and hot pants, bought to go to our first disco with Lynne Atkins, shuffling around in a circle around our handbags to *Hey Girl, Don't Bother Me*.

The family has changed since the death of Nan and the divorces of Aunty Eileen and Uncle Charlie. They drift out of our lives and we do not see our dear cousins Dean, Tracey and Marie for many years. But there are additions to the family. Uncle John marries my pretty Auntie Carol from Bearwood in 1971, the year after Nan's death, and we all turn up at the Registry Office on Broad Street in freezing winter weather. Later that year, my cousin Jason is born. And Auntie Margaret, after some years of marriage, produces two sons in rapid succession, my cousins Mark and Matthew. My sister and I are teenagers when these little boys are born and are fascinated by the fact that we are now the eldest of our generation. It is this family that now turns up at the house at Christmas, where Mom lays on a huge buffet supper, accompanied by Babycham and Snowballs for the ladies and Watneys Party Seven for the men, and we dance to the records of the year and gather round the telly to watch *Morecambe and Wise*. There are only four of us for Christmas dinner now, and this is preceded by the opening of Christmas presents, still exciting, although now of course we do not believe any more in Father Christmas.

The first Christmas in New John Street West, we get enormous teddies, blue and red, which we christen with the original names of Rudolf (for the red nosed reindeer) and Bluey. These are the last childlike presents we will ever get, and very soon, our soft toys are relegated to the wardrobe and the loft. The very next Christmas, we get transistor radios with headphones, permanently tuned to Radios Caroline and Luxembourg (after a brief flirtation with Tony Blackburn on Radio One, Mom has returned to Radio Two). Hairdryers follow and for me a chemistry set complete with test tubes and a Bunsen Burner, vanity cases from the estate's Avon ladies, and *Aquamanda*, our first perfume. The *Jackie* and *High Chaparral* annuals replace the *Beano* and the *Bunty*. We scan the *Radio Times* and *TV Times* for festive viewing. Dad's present is *Brut 33* aftershave, solely due to the Henry Cooper advertisement ("Splash it all over!").

We listen to Radios Caroline and Luxembourg under the bedclothes at night, with earphones, though I am pleasantly surprised by *A Book at Bedtime* and the plays and classic dramas on BBC Radio Four.

But the best teenage present is our tape recorder – a joint one. It is almost the size of a record player and comes with a microphone. Dad enjoys showing us how to work it. We play back the tape and hear our voices for the first time; my first recorded words when Susie shoves the mike in my face, are "I don't know what to say!" However, we are soon recording whole plays and programmes with Kim Harrison and discovering that the tape is both two-sided and apt to tangle. "Our *voices*," says Susie, appalled, "We sound just like Brummies." It doesn't really go with my script for *The Six Wives of Henry the Eighth*, with me as Henry, and Susie and Kim playing three wives each and all the supporting parts.

When we get our own record player, on which we can play our Marc Bolan records, we suddenly realise that we can have a soundtrack to our recorded dramas, and produce an epic musical version of *Cinderella*, with Kim as Cinderella, me as the Prince, and Susie as everyone else. Less successful are our efforts to get Sarah the Dog to bark for the tape; we console ourselves by rigging up a kind of assault course in the back garden, and training her to jump it.

New Year's Day is finally a holiday (after 1974), and Mom and Dad can have a lie in after an evening at the Mackadown.

Dad has now done both the gardens beautifully and as we lounge there in deckchairs in the summer, playing Monopoly, the old back yard from Guildford Street seems very far away. But Dad spends most of his time there in the shed, doing DIY with the assistance of the products of White's Ironmonger's on Summer Lane.

We now no longer go out for days with Mom and Dad on the Bank Holidays. We stay at home while they head off to Ross on Wye and Stourport on Severn to meet their friends, "and sit in the pub all day. How can they enjoy that?" asks Susie, puzzled. But we do sit and watch the telly with them, as apart from our liking for *The Wombles*, we no longer watch children's telly and are happy to sit and watch *Call My Bluff*, *Man about the House*, and *Dad's Army*. Mom's favourite is *Not in Front of the Children*, with Wendy Craig.

Weekends are taken up with visits from Auntie Mary, now bent over double and crippled with arthritis but as cheerful as ever and Uncle Albert, who strolls with Dad over to the Clements Arms. Sundays see the arrival of the Atkins family for tea, Stan, Barbara, Lynne and Andrew. Andrew joins gamely in our board and card games, and pop concerts recorded on the tape recorder. He is our Little Brother.

There are several modern pubs on the estate, The Lamplighter and The King of the Road, and in the precinct The Griffin and The Paddock. There is also the Unity Club on the estate but Mom and Dad think the pubs are getting "a bit rough", a sign of the times, and prefer to meet their mates at the Old Crown and Cushion in Great Barr.

We still go on holiday with Mom and Dad and their friends, and this is now always to Perran Sands in Cornwall, a rather epic journey down the M5 and A30, "where there is always a traffic jam at Indian Queen," grumbles Dad. We miss the days of the farm at Bigbury Court, but Perran Sands with its nightly cabaret suits them very well, as they can sit in the bar all night while we watch the entertainment and invent a romance for Lynne with the camp host, Derek Tandy. There are fewer days on the beach, but we enjoy walking with Mom around the shops at Perranporth and days out at Mevagissey, St Agnes and St Ives, where Mom buys me a china seal in the Seal Sanctuary which I have to this day. And I beg to be taken to Truro, to see the cathedral and Tintagel, where I dream of the stories of King Arthur.

But 1973 dawns rather ominously, because this is the year when I am due to sit my GCE examinations, and if I am lucky, become the first family member ever to enter the Sixth Form.

II

We're in the Sixth!

1973–1975

So 1973 is GCE year, and following the Mocks at Christmas 1972, I am allowed to drop all the sciences, with relief. Lessons now consist almost entirely of revision and past exam papers, and singing and PE are dropped in favour of silent study periods in the library. I ponder my A level choices and choose, for no apparent reason, English Literature, French and Latin. I should in fact have picked RE and History, as Mrs Thorne wants as they are my best subjects, but for some reason I want to improve my languages. Latin might be useful if I ever want to learn Italian, maybe.

There seems to be a silent understanding between Miss Sargeant, the mistresses and me that I will go into the Sixth Form. In fact, I will be the first member of my family not to leave school at the earliest opportunity; even clever David Burke left Gower Street at the age of sixteen and is now doing well as a bank clerk. Margaret McLaney has a job lined up at Chelsea Girl and to my sorrow, Jennie and Lesley are leaving; they too have jobs in shops lined up.

Months of revision culminate in the examinations. We are taking the joint Matriculation Board examinations and following Assembly every morning we are led silently into the Hall, where rows of desks and chairs are laid out facing the big wooden clock. Some of the smaller groups, such as Latin and RE, are held in classrooms. Due to sensible management by the School, they pass without incident, except when Mrs Gregory (English) notices me during

Maths rather helplessly filling my fountain pen in the inkwell and dropping large blots on the blotting paper, to express my general hopelessness.

Once the exams are over, we are free to enjoy the end of term, with Sports Day, the Flower Show and the Fry Cup Tennis tournament, but of course we of the Upper Fifth have no lessons as we have nothing to learn. We are sent off to do community service and I anxiously change beds and serve tea at Dudley Road Hospital. And right at the end of term, we all troop out into the playground for the school photograph, precariously perched on benches, even the Sixth Form in uniform, while Miss Sargeant grins at the front, surrounded by the staff. The eventual photograph is so long in length that it comes in a special round cardboard poster box.

The staff come up trumps with an end of term talent show, during which it turns out that Mr Scarborough (American, History) is an excellent piano player. But the last day of term is a sad one, with some girls in tears, and those who are leaving having their blue shirts and final editions of *The Beacon* autographed by the rest of us.

While waiting for the GCE results to come out in August, I have a summer of working at Littlewood's ahead of me. We have two weeks at Perran Sands and I have my trips to the library armed with a Sixth Form reading list. I spend much more time borrowing books for myself as reading is now my main hobby, with Susie off playing with Kim Harrison every day. The pony, boarding school and ballet books of my childhood are now far behind me. I now read every Jean Plaidy book in the library, all of Anya Seton, being especially thrilled by *Katherine*, and pass on to Georgette Heyer's Regency romances, the historical novelist Margaret Irwin, Mazo de la Roche, Annemarie Selinko's *Desiree*, and Daphne du Maurier. After staring at the two volume paperback edition of *Forever Amber* in Hudson's Bookshop for some weeks, I do dare to request it from the library and tear through it. "I've heard that's a bit racy," says Mom when she sees me reading it. "It's not," I say defiantly and untruthfully.

She only shrugs. In a splendid display of tolerance, my parents have never censored anything we read. They are shocked, however, when I pay thirteen and sixpence for a paperback copy of *Gone with the Wind*, just after we have been to see it at the Gaumont (which has gone all retro after the long run of *The Sound of Music. Camelot, Dr Doolittle* and *My Fair Lady* are not as successful, although the rather dreadful *Song of Norway* is. The world of film is not too good in the 70s). The family just doesn't believe in spending money on books; even Dad and Floss, the readers, only borrow from the public library.

There are no teenage sections in the library – there are no teenage books. My Auntie Carol, who works in Bearwood Library, does give me a book called *Fifteen*, by Beverly Cleary. I read this novel of American teenagers with huge enjoyment, but it is too far removed from the British experience to be of help. However, it does make me think of my appearance, of which I am fed up.

In fact, my spots have cleared up naturally, which encourages me to draw some of my hard earned money out of the Halifax in Colmore Row and go for a professional makeup lesson at a small hairdresser's on Great Hampton Row, next to the Little Brown Jug. The lady also plucks my heavy eyebrows, amid many a squeal from me. This is all I can afford, but I do push the boat out by having my ears pierced at Rackham's. I nervously make an appointment at the immaculate beauty salon, full of immaculate women in immaculate pink overalls, and me gauche in my school coat. The lady is however very kind, informs me that my ears will be sore for several days after (which they are), gives me a bottle of surgical spirit to dab on my ears, and two free pairs of sleepers and studs. "At least Mom isn't here," says Susie who has come with me to ride the moving staircase and gape at the lift boys, and we giggle.

Since beginning afternoons at Great Hampton Street, Mom has ceased being a shop steward, and we hear no more of her battles with Management. However, she does need a Cause and the Cause is the wearing of fur which centres around, in her case, the abolition of the fur department at Rackham's. Susie and I do take a peep at it, and are not impressed at the sight of the chained down coats. A year or so ago, we got off the bus after school on Corporation Street, thinking of nipping into C&A, when Susie grabs my arm, "Look!"

There outside Rackham's is an anti-fur wearing demo and right in the middle of it is our mom, fag hanging from lips, as she waves a placard telling us that it takes forty dumb animals to make a coat, but only one to wear it.

"Run!" whispers Susie.

"I dunno," I say doubtfully. "I mean, think of that baby seal poster. I think she's right, I had nightmares after that."

"So do I, but we are surrounded by girls from King Ed's and that's our mom!"

And so we scarper in a very cowardly way.

I have realised that there is nothing I can do about my height, five feet two is all I will ever reach, and Susie now towers over me and pats my head in a very condescending manner. However, with the worst of adolescence over, our fights too are over, which is a relief as she tended to win.

But my weight is too much for my height and I decide to do something about it. I stop eating biscuits, cakes and chocolate to Mom's chagrin, and tell her I don't want any more puddings. No more Picnics, Lion Bars, Caramacs and Golden Cups. I walk everywhere, including into town every day for Littlewood's, and up to the libraries at Aston and Spring Hill. I spend hours on the estate on my bike, riding around with Kim and Susie, and I'm down at Newtown Baths every week with Uncle John, if not playing tennis in the car park, banging the tennis ball against the wall and watched by the old ladies in Thornton House.

At the end of the holidays, shortly before school starts, I draw out some more money and head for C&A's Gear Cellar. There is no school uniform in the Sixth Form and my wardrobe is looking a bit bare for everyday use so I even treat myself to a couple of items from Chelsea Girl, Richard Shops and Miss Selfridge. To my delight, I find that I have dropped an entire size, down to size 12, and that night I parade my new clothes to an open-mouthed Mom. Dad comes in as I waltz around in a new C&A party frock. "Well," he says staring, "blue is certainly your colour." And after years of being a plump and plain teenager, that's as good as it gets. I'm passable.

Only one thing left to do. For years, I have worn my long, straight hair tied back at school; it reaches my waist but unless I wear a rather girlish headband every day, it's going to be a nuisance. I consult Mom. "Colour first," she says, "and then a trip to Auntie Margaret's."

From Snape's the Chemist, using the Make Up Chance, she buys a bottle of Rimmel Hair Colour labelled Deep Auburn, applies the rather foul smelling mixture to my hair and combs it out after half hour, at which time I have become a redhead.

Very nice," says Mom proudly. "We need to touch it up every six weeks."

"I want mine done too," says Susie – after years of being a blonde bombshell, she has become, like me, an English Mouse.

"I don't think Miss Sargeant would approve," says Mom doubtfully. "Maybe wait till you are in the Sixth Form too."

Susie pulls a face, but that's not the end of it. She uses some of her Woolworth's money to buy herself a mysterious bottle labelled Nestle's Beautiful Blonde, and applies it one Sunday afternoon when Mom and Dad are at the cemetery, with the help of Kim Harrison. Kim comes running for me.

"Grace, Grace, come quick! Susie's hair!"

I rush into the living room where Susie is bent over an orange plastic bowl. Her hair is turning blonder as I look at it, minute by minute.

"Get her over the sink! Wash it off!"

Despite our best efforts, by the time Mom gets home, Susie looks rather like Jean Harlow.

"Oh, my God," says Mom faintly, while Dad dissolves into laughter.

"She's blonder than Marilyn."

And Susie's hair is indeed almost *white*. She is in tears.

"I told you," scolds Mom. "I mean, Nestle doesn't even make good chocolate." She is still loyal to Cadbury's.

The next afternoon finds us on the Midland Red on our way up to Sutton Coldfield, to see what Auntie Margaret can do. She runs a salon from a room in her house, and it's a chance for Mom to coo over Mark and Matthew. Clucking over Susie's hair, she applies a honey blonde toner that at least returns Susie to some of her former glory without being so noticeably platinum, and then it's my turn.

"I want a feather cut," I say.

"Oh Grace, I don't think that will do for you. Your hair just wants to be straight. Even as I'm brushing it, I can see that."

We compromise on a shoulder length bob with a side parting, which I wear to this very day, after one or two brief and unsuccessful flirtations with permanent waves.

My final shopping expedition is to the Co-op for some *Aquamanda* scent and deodorant, and to Grey's for some cheap and trendy jewellery made by Corocraft. And then, after years of agony, Dad takes me to the Dental Hospital for the removal of my brace. My teeth aren't wonderful still, but they no longer stick out at right angles.

Hair, clothes, make up... I'm ready for the Sixth Form.

One morning in August, I'm fast asleep at 7am when Mom and Dad burst into my bedroom, waving a postcard (the post comes very early).

"It's your results!"

Through a blur of sleep, I see that I have six GCEs, all in Grade Ones and Twos, apart of course from Maths, which nobody kindly mentions. Shortly after this, the letter from King Edward's arrives, inviting me to the first day of the Sixth Form.

When I do start the Sixth Form, it is because we are actually better off now than we have been for a long time. Susie and I both have Saturday jobs. Mom is afternoons at Great Hampton Street, supervisor of her line, and she runs a *Burlington* catalogue on the estate; we love looking through its highly scented pages when it arrives twice a year. Most of her customers are the old ladies in the high rise flats on the estate. She still hasn't got a bank account and pays her money in at the Post Office in the Precinct.

Dad is doing very well. All those years of studying at the Open University have paid off, he is now toolroom Manager at Tucker's, and the ever faithful Johnnie Murray is now his foreman. Dad has got an office, a phone of his own, and he proudly brings the Tucker internal phone book home with his listing for his own phone and office, and photos of his promotion in the Tucker's magazine, *Insight*.

At home, this new found wealth expresses itself in a new Music Centre with stereo sound, and Susie and I get the Dansette upstairs. We have our own collection of singles by The Monkees and Slade, and scorn Mom and Dad's Music for Pleasure Easy Listening LPs (£2.99). The only time we unite on music is for the Eurovision Song Contest. Dad is very taken with Dana singing *All Kinds of Everything* in 1970 ("Isn't she beautiful?").

Moreover, carried away by their new prestige, Dad and Johnnie decide to take up golf. It is, after all, the sport of the young executive who wears a suit, not a blue overall, for work. This does mean that Dad will need some basic golfing equipment and clothing. Despite his promotion, he is cautious.

"Maybe the Green Shield stamps will pay for some of it," says Mom hopefully.

Ever since the Co-op divvy expired, we have been collecting Green Shield stamps in little books. When we have collected what seems to be 1000s, we go off to the Green Shield Stamp Shop under the Rotunda, and get a set of screwdrivers. But the stamps are nowhere near what Dad needs for golfing equipment, and eventually he splashes out on basic equipment and clothing from Harry Parkes in Corporation Street. Harry, of course, used to play for the Villa.

This is the beginning of an obsession for Dad and Johnnie, out on the Municipal golf courses every Saturday, and in the summer straight after work. There is no booking system, so on Boxing Day and New Year's Day, they join the queue in their cars at 4am, sleeping for a couple of hours till the courses open. Eventually, they decide to splash out on membership of Great Barr Golf Club. Mom is aghast at the price, but there's no doubt Dad loves it, and Susie and I are ecstatic because we no longer need to buy him pens, hankies and socks for birthdays and Christmases. We can catch the bus up the Walsall Road to Great Barr and buy golf clubs, waterproofs and golfing gloves from the pro shop.

In September 1973, I get up one fine autumn morning, dress myself in a new purple blouse with a wing collar and a black skirt (I'm not yet daring enough to wear trousers to school), and throw my sandwiches and a pencil case into a shoulder bag (my trusty old satchel died a natural death). Susie, fully clad in school uniform, has already left, scowling, so I find myself late and puffing up Rose Hill Road. Ahead of me, strolling casually, is Theresa, who was in Z with me.

"Wotcha running for?"

"Think we're late, Tess!"

Theresa laughs. "We're not late. No Prayers for the Sixth Form. Wait in the playroom or the Brew Room and go into Assembly."

I'm not sorry to miss prayers and hymns and we go into the Brew Room, a small former classroom which is now a Sixth Form drop in, named after a former Headmistress who is reputed to haunt it. It is undoubtedly very cold in there, and most of the Sixth Form prefer a larger Common Room at the side of the school (where it is possible to smuggle in boys from Handsworth Grammar). We compare GCE results and our choices: some of the girls are making last minute switches. Also, we eye up each other's costume choices.

The Upper and Lower Sixth take their places in the back two rows of the Assembly Hall, which looks as glorious as ever as Miss Sargeant beams from the platform at the new intake, who look very small to us. I am reminded of myself, five years ago.

After assembly, the new Lower Sixth assembles in the Sixth Form block, which is in fact no more than the upper floor of the dining block. Choices are finalised, the rules and regulations read, and timetables given out. We are ecstatic to find that we have free time; this is the first time in five years that I won't be continuously on the go from nine till four.

In truth, it would never have occurred to any of us to go anywhere else for Sixth Form education. The King Edwards Schools are hanging onto grammar school education by a thread. In 1965, Birmingham City Council voted to abolish grammar schools and since 1970 the King Edwards Schools have been involved in a running battle to maintain grammar school, and finally independent status. Susie was in the last year to sit the eleven plus examination. It is now extremely difficult to get in. But it seems sad to me to remember all those children who did not pass the eleven plus, and were relegated to the secondary moderns. And by now, many of the former Grammar Schools, such as George Dixon and Marsh Hill, are Comprehensives.

After all this, it is break. I am sitting with Lorna Hitchin and Janet Buet, who I know from Jennie's class, two dark girls called Jill and Yvonne, and quiet Kerry from Z.

"Let's have a break together," I suggest. After all, I need new friends.

We buy ourselves a drink from the school tuck shop and some iced buns, and take them to the Sixth Form Common Room at the side of the school. We find that we're all doing English Literature and French, I'm the only one doing Latin, and Janet and Yvonne are doing Geography.

Jill tosses her head. "I failed my GCEs, so I'm retaking them in something called the Remove." She produces a packet of cigarettes from her bag. We goggle in awe.

The rest of the day consists of meeting our new teachers and finding out the A Level curriculum. I have several teachers for English. Mrs Tunstall, elegant and grey haired, is taking us for *Mansfield Park*, Chaucer's *Prologue* and *Nonne Preeste's Tale*. Mrs Gough is young with flashing eyes and long dark hair which she tosses dramatically as she expounds the virtues of W. B. Yeats and Wilfred Owen. Mrs Gregory is mild and red-haired, and takes us through *Antony and Cleopatra* and *Richard the Second*.

We still have Mrs Dolman, formerly Miss Allen, for French. Mr Dolman has left as he is training for the Ministry. With Mrs Dolman we read the short stories of Guy de Maupassant and the *Souvenirs d'Enfance* of Marcel Pagnol which I rather like.

We have another teacher, Mr Aldridge, who teaches us language from a book of prose translations, but his heart obviously lies in the Existentialism he expounds through Jean Paul Sartre and Andre Gide's *The Counterfeiters*. His efforts are admirable, but we are 16 year old girls interested in pop music, clothes and make up.

"I can explain Existentialism by climbing out the window of the Sixth Form block, standing on the sill, and deliberating whether I have the right to throw myself off," he offers.

"It might make things more exciting," we mutter.

Mr Aldridge has a habit of standing with his back to the chalkboard, which means that his trendy cord jacket is usually covered with white powder. But this doesn't stop Pat Ruston from falling for him and gazing at him with dreamy eyes. He is, after all, a novelty in a school of mainly mistresses. "I've heard his first name is Grisewald," she announces, which seems very unlikely, but Grisewald he becomes and remains. Staff first names are unknown and exciting.

As we still speak French with Brummie accents, we meet once a week with a genuinely French *assistante* for conversation. Arlette wears a beret in what we see as a stereotyped French style and is obsessed with French cinema, showing us her photos of rather glamorous French film stars. Monsieur Bensheikh (schoolgirl humour: Mr Binsik), is Algerian and preaches the Revolution. He is dark, scowling, moody and wears jeans and a black T shirt. He loves Camus and hates De Gaulle. There is not much discussion of the pen of my aunt being in the garden.

By some amazing chance, I am the only girl who put down to do Latin, and in any other school, it simply wouldn't run. But this is King Edward's and Latin is run by the formidable Miss Boggis. Week after week, I sit alone in the classroom as she takes me through the mysteries of Lucretius' *De Rerum Natura*, the boredom of Cicero's letters, and the very exciting poetry of Catullus, in a schoolgirl edition with rows of asterisks for the censored lines.

Our group soon establishes its priorities. "Coles Notes for all the English texts," I dictate, "They've got them in WH Smith's." We pool the money from our Saturday jobs and Janet trots off for multiple copies, plus Neville Coghill's Penguin Classics translation of *The Canterbury Tales*, much looked down on by Mrs Tunstall for inaccuracies. French takes a bit longer. Lorna, who intends to read French at University, triumphantly returns from the Midland Education with several copies of Gide's *The Counterfeiters*, costing, to our horror, fifty pence (ten shillings) each. "I don't even *like* the book," mutters Yvonne.

Hudson's Bookshop yields The *Selected Short Stories of Guy de Maupassant*, which contains most of the selection we are reading. Sartre and Pagnol prove much more difficult to track down until, poking around in the depths of the 400 languages section of Central Library which is rarely visited, I find mouldering old translations called *Dirty Hands* and *The Days Were Too Short*, which haven't been out for twenty years. Feeling guilty and in a tremendous breach of copyright, I borrow them, photocopy them on my lunch hour and circulate them. Voltaire's *Lettres Philosophiques* prove impossible to find a translation of, in the days before the internet. "Not surprising, they're so boring," complains Janet. We delegate Lorna to read them all and communicate the contents to the rest of us.

I'm on my own when it comes to Latin. The school Reference Library mysteriously yields an almost word for word translation of the equally mysterious Lucretius. It is with bitter resentment that I fork out my hard earned Saturday job money on a Penguin *Selected Letters of Cicero*, because I have developed an almost pathological hatred of Cicero. But I don't mind paying twenty-five pence for a selection of Catullus' poetry I also find in Hudson's. Firstly, I have developed a huge liking for the poems, which results in a visit to Verona, his birth place, nearly fifty years later. Secondly, the translation has got all the naughty bits cut out of my schoolgirl Loeb.

"I wish I was doing Latin," laments Lorna when I relate all this to her.

"Why on earth? There's only two of us and we could sit in the Brew Room, but Miss Boggis insists on a classroom. And she makes me use an exercise book and fountain pen."

Every other class lets us use folders and biros, though this often results in panic when we lose bits of paper.

"Well, I now need to do Latin to O Level to sit the Oxbridge exam, so I need to do it in a year. You should sit the Oxbridge too," explains Lorna.

I am doubtful about this. I will be the first person in my family to go to University, and Oxbridge seems like a bridge too far. Moreover, I have another problem. School says I need to resit Maths. With Jill, I sit through the GCE Maths resits in November and June, failing both.

"I think," I say tearfully to Miss Naish, "if you put me in for CSE, I might pass that." Miss Naish is shocked – King Ed's doesn't do CSE – but as it's hopeless, she concedes and I do in fact, relieved of trigonometry, algebra and logarithms, sail through the CSE.

I spend two very happy years in the Sixth Form. I enjoy all my subjects and the quality of teaching is excellent. As we can now miss Prayers, all of the Sixth Form has cheerfully and pragmatically decided it is agnostic and can thus spend an extra fifteen minutes in bed every morning. We can wear our own clothes and attempt to outdo each other in the products of Chelsea Girl and Miss Selfridge; we think we look lovely in our flared trousers, tank tops, ponchos and platform soles. We have plenty of free time which we can spend in the library, the Brew Room or the Sixth Form Common Room. We don't have to have school dinners; we can bring sandwiches or legitimately go to the chippie on Soho Road, to the envy of the younger girls, who are forbidden to leave school at lunch time.

School decides to broaden our horizons with a series of theatre trips. Sadly, we are banned from group visits to Birmingham Repertory Theatre because we were taken to see a production of *Macbeth* when we were doing it for GCE, which we assumed was being played as a black comedy and we were in stitches throughout. In fact, it wasn't being played for laughs and the Manager of the Rep wrote a furious letter to Miss Sargeant saying that we were the worst behaved school ever to visit the Rep. Miss Sargeant read this out in Assembly and the Upper Fifth was fit to die.

We have to go further afield, so Mrs Gregory resignedly takes us on a coach trip to Stoke on Trent, where we witness an in the round production of

Antony and Cleopatra. Sadly, just as Antony plunges his sword into his breast, an ambulance roars past outside, klaxon blaring and the entire audience collapses in laughter.

Much more successful is a coach trip to see *Richard the Second* in Stratford upon Avon and for the first time ever, I can see what Shakespeare is like if done well.

Mr Aldridge, the Existentialist, takes us off one evening to see a play called *No Exit* by his hero Jean-Paul Sartre at Birmingham University. As soon as the play begins, there are anxious glances up and down the row of Sixth Form A Level French.

"They're speaking in French," mutters Pat. "I can't understand a word."

And indeed, there is a difference between the French they speak and our Birmingham accented schoolgirl French. Moreover, we are generally, reading the texts in translation (learning a few subtle essay quotations in French). We did not even know that the play was actually called *Huis Clos.*

Yvonne and I sign up for the Duke of Edinburgh's Bronze Award. For some reason, we have to spend a day yomping across Cannock Chase with huge packs on our back. Dad gives me a tip; "I had to do that when I was doing National Service with the Marines. They had us yomping across Dartmoor. I was wandering along when a bus stopped and the driver said, 'Mate, free rides for the forces.' Just pretended to be a bit out of breath when I got back to base."

Sadly, no bus appears on Cannock Chase, but an exhausted Yvonne and I do stop halfway, and sit down for a rest on a wall which has apparently stood there since the time of the Romans. It promptly falls over and a farmer writes a furious letter to school, after which we decide to give up the D of E.

As part of the community service, I have signed up to visit an old lady on the estate who lives in one of the maisonettes. Her name is Beatrice and she is in her eighties, virtually deaf and toothless. Because she seems to enjoy my visits, I don't think I can give them up and I dutifully visit until one night I go in and poor Beatrice is dead in bed. I run to tell Violet next door. It is the first time I have ever seen a dead body.

My social life is also much improved now I have a group of friends. We spend hours wandering around the Art Gallery on Sundays, admiring the Pre-Raphaelites and Impressionists, and listening to the piano in the Edwardian tea rooms. We take the bus out to Blakesley Manor, Sarehole Mill and Birmingham Botanical Gardens. When not being cultured, we drink Britvic Orange juices in Fanny's on Great Charles Street and play the jukebox with what we hope are more sophisticated tracks than glam rock: David Bowie, Stevie Wonder and Led Zeppelin. We are trying to forget that we used to like Sweet, Slade and the Bay City Rollers.

This selective forgetfulness doesn't apply to a wistful visit to *The Wombles, the Musical* at the Alexandra, from which we emerge rather guiltily and decide to try *Little Women* the week after. This is interrupted by an American heckler ranting loudly about Richard Nixon and Watergate, during which the cast carry gamely on as the theatre staff shuffle him off to the Exit.

"I think we need to go more highbrow," announces Lorna. There's a Young Rep club at the Rep. If we join that, we can watch the rehearsals and we get cheap tickets." This is what we do and we get to see productions of *Man and Superman*, *The Recruiting Officer* and *Vivat! Vivat! Regina* which I enjoy hugely.

The Odeons on New Street and the Queensway are now our cinemas of choice, and it is here that we see *The Sting* and, greatly daring, *Love Story*. Paul Newman replaces Captain Scarlet and Troy Tempest as my true love, and Mom allows me to have a huge poster of him put up over my bed.

Lorna is inspired by all these cultural activities to start a Sixth Form culture club, which kicks off with a guitar concert at Birmingham Town Hall, but much more exciting than this, offers the opportunity for us to mingle with the opposite sex in the shape of other boys' grammar schools. The opposite sex is something that fascinates the Sixth Form – and in particular the boys of Handsworth Grammar and King Edward's Aston, seen as our natural prey.

It begins with the Sixth Form paperback library, which is a small bookcase in the Sixth Form block kept locked unless we ask for the key. This is possibly because it contains a copy of *Lady Chatterley's Lover*. I read this, dutifully pass it around and we all agree that it is very dull. Much more exciting is a book that one of the girls brings in called *Doctors' Wives*, which she found under her Dad's pillow.

I find all this is a bit terrifying and I have good reason.

I've stopped going to the Youth Club at St George's since I passed sixteen. Dad had started walking me back from there because he thinks the estate is getting rough and one night I'm waiting outside for Dad and the Rev Geoffrey Brown is locking up.

"I'll wait here till Dad turns up."

"Good night," he calls cheerily. He disappears inside.

A man walks past. I can smell beery fumes and he snickers, "Get yer tits out for the lads!" And he lunges out, grabs one of my small breasts and lurches off into the darkness, laughing. I am fourteen years old. I stand in shock, till Dad arrives a couple of minutes later, pleased that he is protecting me. But he didn't, he couldn't. And I never told him. I didn't tell the vicar. I told nobody.

A year later I am due to go to the Odeon New Street one Sunday afternoon with Lynne Atkins, to see a film called *A Doll's House* but Lynne doesn't feel well, and so I go alone as I want to see the film. I sit alone in the middle of a row – not many are there – and halfway through, a man comes up and sits next to me. He stares at the screen. He is breathing heavily. One hand is under his mac. After a moment, I feel his hand on my leg, moving up and down. As with the Youth Club incident, I am frozen for a moment. As his breathing gets more rapid, I get up quickly and flee to the rear of the Odeon, where I thankfully sit myself very close to an usherette. But I don't tell her. I don't tell anyone. Because nobody saw it. Because they would deny it.

After these incidents I never go to the Youth Club again, or to the pictures alone.

And that was wrong. I had the right to stand alone outside the Youth Club, I had the right to sit alone in the pictures. They did not have the right to do what they did to a young girl and so I was well able to believe #metoo. We never spoke up because they did it so that there was no proof. And so I am not too enthusiastic about learning about sex. But like most of the Sixth Form, I would like a boyfriend.

School places our romances, with a frown, under a banner labelled Silliness. Silliness includes the Ouija craze which sweeps the Upper School, with glasses, hand-lettered alphabets and girls claiming to levitate. Silliness is the excessive religious ecstasies some of the girls experience, wearing large crucifixes and speaking of God as though he were their next door neighbour, Godfrey (God for short). Silliness is carving Pete Duel and David Cassidy on the inside of your desk lid with your compass and taping photos of *Alias Smith and Jones* to it.

Some of the girls venture to Cradley Heath speedway in search of lads (there are rumours that you can meet skinheads there, which is very daring). This is a bit far for my group, so we decide to concentrate our efforts on Lorna's Culture Club, the Silver Blades Ice Rink and the Friday night discos. We all feel the need for a bloke who isn't simply a poster on your bedroom wall.

Culture Club begins with a debate with Yardley Boys, but sadly doesn't lead to any romance. School plays its part; they decide that it is OK if we have a Friday night disco with Handsworth Grammar and King Edward's Aston.

We turn up in all the splendour of Miss Selfridge's finest, and dance in circles to the innocuous Carpenters and Bread around our handbags (Black Sabbath, our local band, are banned, as are Led Zeppelin). The lads stand around the walls, interspersed with the teachers, who are checking that we don't go outside a) with one of the boys and b) for a smoke.

Another romantic hope is that we might meet a boy at the Silver Blades Skating Rink. Now that we are in the Sixth, we are relieved of the necessity to play games, but we can spend Friday afternoons at the Silver Blades Ice Rink, in company with King Edward's Aston. In fact, most of the girls bunk off to the Kardomah Coffee Bar, where they might meet more sophisticated men, but Janet, Lorna, Yvonne and I decide to give the Silver Blades a whirl. I am, in fact, sufficiently carried away to check the *Birmingham Evening Mail* For Sale columns for a pair of skating boots Size 4. When I find some, price £5, Dad resignedly takes me up to the Castle Vale estate to get them.

It's of no use; Janet, Yvonne and I stumble around the edge while Lorna pirouettes and arabesques in the centre.

These futile efforts do pay off a bit. For a start Lorna meets, through a Culture Club visit to a classical guitar concert at the Town Hall, a very sophisticated Music student called Rupert ("Daaarlings!"). Lorna and Rupert embark on a programme of CBSO visits and play guitar duets together. He does look a bit like her idol, Robert Powell.

In the meantime, Janet has set her sights on Alfred, a boy from Handsworth Grammar she meets at the Ice Rink, and shyly they waltz hand in hand around the edge to the Skaters' Waltz.

"Nobody of our age is called Alfred," Yvonne says scornfully.

"It's his grandad's name," says Janet defensively.

"Their passion melts the ice!" I shriek, which reduces Lorna, Yvonne and Kerry to fits of giggles, while Janet glares.

"He's taking me to the Albion next Saturday," she says even more defensively.

"I wouldn't go there if I were paid..."

This leaves Yvonne and I at a loose end, still shuffling hopelessly round the Friday night discos, without dates, even though I have splashed out and bought a long yellow and black dress from Oasis and a navy blue midi skirt and frilly white blouse from (daringly) a boutique off New Street. I am convinced that I look the height of sophistication.

Then, one Saturday morning, Yvonne rings me from Wimbush's at the Central Library.

"You remember the fair haired boy I was dancing with last night?"

I can indeed remember them shuffling around to the strains of Paper Lace.

"Well, his name is Clive Farmer but they call him Pitchfork at school. You know, farmers. Anyway, he wants to take me to see *Murder on the Orient Express* at the Elite on Soho Road next weekend – if it's on – and he's got a mate who'll take you!"

"What's his name?" I ask feebly, aware of everyone in the staff room listening.

"Oh, John Spade, but they call him Digger. You know, builders."

I have indeed noticed that the boys of Handsworth Grammar are usually known by quite derogatory nicknames. Any similar attempts at our School, such as Goofy, Fatty and Spotty, are frowned on horribly by the mistresses. But I am excited by my date. I rush out at lunchtime and buy myself some Boots 17 makeup and a new pair of dangly earrings. I really don't know what to wear and drift around Gear Cellar, Richard Shops, Dorothy Perkins and Chelsea Girl till I find an orange mini dress (£5).

Yvonne and I scan the *Birmingham Evening Mail* anxiously till the listings come out on Thursday. "Yes, it's on. See you there at seven." There is no problem with Mom and Dad, who are thrilled that I have a date, although the length of time I am spending in the freezing bathroom annoys them. I am making daring efforts to remove under arm and leg hair with Mom's foul smelling Immac.

"I thought *Aquamanda* was bad enough," groans Dad. "Why can't women just shave, like blokes?" He is equally revolted by the stench of my Boots Clearaway with Clay face pack, which glows an alarming green in the dark and makes Susie shriek.

Saturday night sees me bumping up the Soho Road on the No 70, dreaming of love, romance, marriage, children, a little part-time job in a cake shop and a semi-detached in Great Barr. I am smothered in *Occur!* talcum powder and accompanied by waves of Avon's *Pretty Peach* skin perfume, both purchased from Balbir, who runs an Avon catalogue at school.

Digger turns out to be not much taller than me, with brown hair and an anxious expression. However, in a splendid gesture, the lads pay for us to go in. Sitting absorbed in the adventures of Albert Finney et al, I suddenly become aware of a hand on my knee. I freeze. It is the man in the Odeon all over again. I knock Digger's hand off and he doesn't try again but he does buy me a tub of ice cream in the interval. Yvonne and Pitchfork are getting on splendidly.

"They want us to go round to Pitchfork's this Sunday afternoon and play records, so bring some," Yvonne tells me on Monday break as we blow bubbles in our lemonade.

For this date, and much to Mom's horror, I elect to wear flared trousers and a tank top ("Girls just aren't girls anymore!"). I arrive armed with Gary Puckett's *Young Girl* and the Shangri Las' *Leader of the Pack*, which I also think is the height of sophistication and we settle down to listen to an afternoon of Mud, Wizzard, Slade, and the Bay City Rollers. At some point, Pitchfork and Digger make their moves and we fight them off.

Rather oddly, my alliance with Digger lasts a few months. He is, in fact, as desperate as I am to have a date and to be able to say at school, "My girlfriend/ my boyfriend." It's an arrangement. We can arrange to meet at the Kardomah, at Fanny's Great Charles Street, at the Perry Bar Clifton, till something better comes along. Dad installs a lock on the phone, times our telephone conversations, decrees a curfew, and is standing at the door as Digger walks me up the path, looking up to Heaven as Digger awkwardly kisses me.

None of our romances outlive the A Levels.

At the end of the Lower Sixth year, we sit our mocks and as a reward, are sent on a coach trip to London. For this, we all wear our newly acquired flared trousers and suede coats, and rush around as many of the sights as we can, on our own, without any of the teachers. We are Growing Up.

12

Goodbye to Birmingham

1974–1975

This is what we were waiting for all these years. We are the Upper Sixth. We are Top of the School. "All of the Upper Sixth are prefects," announces Miss Sargeant, although sadly this comes with a lot of awful duties in the playground and play room, clinging to the radiators as we stop the Lower School escaping to somewhere warmer.

Pretty Pat Ruston does not come back. Her father has died and she decided to get a job. She marries shortly after and we attend her winter wedding, extremely envious that someone can be so young and a bride.

Neither is Jill, who has got sick of the Remove and leaves to get a job in Miss Selfridge, where she can drawl fashion recommendations to the customers. She asks Lorna and I for a farewell drink at the Station Hotel off New Street, where we sip our tonic waters, and gaze on awed as she throws back brandy and Babycham. No barman would ever dare ask Jill how old she is. She shows us a magazine called *Cosmopolitan*, which we flick through anxiously, as it seems to be written in another language. It is not the *Jackie*.

The year kicks off as ever with Speech Day, for which in a retro step, we have to turn out in our school uniforms which really don't fit us very well. I am consoled with Miss Tolley's Prize for English and Lorna with the Maurice Lambot prize for French. Susie gets the Janet Hood Memorial Prize for Mathematics, but shocks the Bailiff of the Foundation by announcing she will spend the book token on the *Alias Smith and Jones Annual*. But this is my last

Speech Day. I drink in the sight of our glorious hall, the rows of girls in navy blue, the teachers in their robes, the Bailiff and the other officials on the flower-decked platform, Miss Sargeant in the great wooden Headmistress's chair (The Throne), the coat of arms of the Tudors, *Dieu et mon Droit,* emblazoned on the wall. The singing of the school anthem and the reciting of the Founder's Prayer. The school orchestra and the school choir. All for the last time.

The 12th October is the birthday of our founder Edward the Sixth, who gazes down at us piously from the front of the hall. He is indeed blessed amongst us, as we get a day off on his birthday. However, the Upper Sixth are expected to attend the Founder's Day Service at St Martin's in the Bull Ring, the foundation church, with the other King Edward's Schools, announces Miss Sargeant.

We all groan, but in the end we are again impressed by the beauty of one of Birmingham's oldest churches, the massed ranks of the King Edwards Schools, the Bailiff and the staff of the Foundation in all their glory, again the singing of the anthem and the saying of the Founder's Prayer. We feel proud to be grammar school girls. Moreover, we are released afterwards into Birmingham City Centre and after lunch at Drucker's, spend a happy afternoon in Hudson's Bookshop and WH Smith record department.

As this is our A Level year, there are no school trips, but because we are reading Wilfred Owen, we are taken on a coach trip to the Imperial War Museum to see *All Quiet on the Western Front,* from which we emerge with reddened eyes, as we usually do in any case from Mrs Gough's Wilfred Owen sessions.

It is Mrs Gough who enrols the Upper Sixth into a Flag Day organised by her husband Roddy, who turns out to be as dramatic as she is, also with flowing hair and scarf. Unfortunately, it snows on the designated day and Lorna and I spend hours freezing outside the Rotunda, shaking our Lifeboats tins. When we stagger back to the office for lunch, we are practically blue with cold.

"Should have worn wellies, like Mom said, instead of these useless Chelsea Girl plastic boots, no warmth at all," I mutter.

With a toss of his shiny hair and a flick of his artistic scarf, Roddy wants to send us out again, as our takings are so meagre, but Mrs Gough intervenes.

"Roddy, those girls are blue with cold!"

We escape, thankfully, to the warmth of Birmingham Art Gallery and hot soup in the Edwardian Tea Rooms. The impressionists and Pre Raphaelites are great favourites here, but we think that the stuffed birds and animals, and the T Rex which roars if you push a button, are beginning to look a bit tatty.

Mrs Tunstall has retired and is replaced by Miss James, who takes a reluctant Upper Sixth English Literature thorough Marlow's *Edward the Second*. We can't quite work out what Edward is doing with Gaveston.

Christmas is dismally preceded by the Mocks, in which we all do quite well. We are beginning to think of The Future.

Susie and I have saved our Saturday job and overtime money for what we think is the Best Christmas Present Ever for Mom and Dad. It is a colour TV from Radio Rentals. There is of course no way we can hide this from them, as the two workmen stagger in on Christmas Eve with it, but we do tie a coloured bow around it.

"I can't believe it," says Mom, staring. "They're all *orange*."

This is the same as the family photos, suddenly blooming in colour since Dad swapped the Box Brownie for a Kodak, but since he has not discovered the flash yet, we have orange skins and red eyes in photos. Dad does indeed have to fiddle around with the controls before we have our first Christmas in colour. The old black and white TV will go with me to University, with a wire coat hanger as an aerial. But generally, Mom and Dad are thrilled that they can watch *Kojak, The Six Million Dollar Man,* and *Columbo* in colour; detective dramas are replacing Westerns on telly as preferred viewing.

Lorna and I are daring enough to book tickets for a New Year's Eve party at the Locarno in Birmingham City Centre. I wear what I consider to be a very sophisticated black floral two piece from Dorothy Perkins, which makes me look quite eighteen (two months off). The only problem is that I keep tripping over the hem. At midnight, after shuffling around our handbags to Mud, Sweet and the Bay City Rollers, we get kissed by loads of boys, which is thrilling, and share a taxi to avoid questing around to find a Night Service bus, outside Grey's every hour on the hour.

The New Year starts with Careers interviews and we have a visit from the Careers Service. I stroll into the freezing Brew Room, well prepared. "Well, I want to be a football journalist," I tell the Careers Officer confidently. "I've been watching *Match of the Day* from the start, I read the *Sports Argus* every week, and I go down the Villa. I think I need to do a degree and then maybe a postgrad in journalism, unless I can get to be a trainee on a newspaper." I have in fact just been standing on the drafty terraces of the Holte End with Lorna, who has suddenly developed an interest in football just as hooliganism has become a problem.

The Careers adviser falls about laughing. "I'm sorry," he says when he recovers, "but girls just can't be football journalists. Even if you get into journalism, you'd be writing about sewing, knitting and cookery."

"But I don't like any of them," I say haughtily and flounce out.

Generally, comparing notes, we discover that those of us planning to go to University have been advised to be teachers, social workers and librarians. Those planning to leave school are advised to get a job as a clerk in a bank or Building Society (not a supervisor or Manager). Despite the fact that some of the girls are quite brilliant at Science, nobody is advised to be a doctor: a nurse or a midwife is their fate.

As with me rejecting the idea of Oxbridge (Lorna is the only one to take the exam, sitting alone in the Sixth Form Library), being a doctor or an engineer is a step too far. We are all daughters of working class parents in industry and virtually all of us are the first members of our families to stay on at school. Had we been to a middle class school, we might have come from a tradition of doctors and dentists, but we don't. School is doing its best – they are all working women – but it is baby steps for us.

Miss Sargeant quotes at us something said by Queen Elizabeth the First, the sister of our Pious Founder, "Girls, she said that she was endowed with such qualities that if she were turned out of the realm in her petticoat, she could make shift for herself. That is what we are doing for you. You will always be able to look after yourselves."

Shifts, we discover, are what we call underskirts. Then we all have nightmares about being found strolling down Colmore Row in our petticoats.

We wave off Mrs Dolman on her maternity leave. Her pregnancy has caused a sensation in school, as does her *maternity leave* ("I don't think they like it," she confides in us). We are now at the mercy of Mr Aldridge, but Mrs Dolman has left us pages and pages of handwritten notes, Xeroxed by School.

The girls who are leaving start dutifully applying to banks and building societies and this includes Janet, who gets a job on Bennetts Hill. Kerry manages to get into the Civil Service. Yvonne has decided to go to Teacher Training College, and as there are more colleges by the sea, she ends up at Charlotte Mason at Ambleside, following an epic coach journey for the interview.

Lorna has given up on Oxbridge and, inspired by our London school trips, has decided to go there. As for me, I do not know where to go. It is easy to decide what to read – School simply thinks we should do our best subject, which is English Literature for me and French for Lorna, because we usually win the annual prizes. There was a smaller range of subjects in those days, all academic, and none as I remember with the word Studies in the title.

While I am pondering this, Lorna and I are filling in our polytechnic applications for Librarianship. There is a rather unfair idea that you need a back-up if you don't get the grades needed for university and the polytechnics, which offer excellent vocational qualifications, are that back up. We travel by train (and this is very thrilling) to Liverpool, Manchester and Newcastle on Tyne, where the very nice people offer us places and probably realise we will never be going there.

University applications, unlike polytechnic, are done through a system called the Universities Central Council on Admissions (UCCA). This is a form that is filled in with the five universities of your choice in turn, and it is rumoured that they are using something called a *Computer* to process them. After some anxious scanning of the UCCA Handbook, I choose Aberystwyth (English and Librarianship), and Nottingham, Leicester, Durham and Warwick for English.

"Durham won't even look at your application if you don't put them first," predicts Lorna and she proves to be right. Mom, of course, wants me to apply to Birmingham. But I don't. I am ready to go.

I now embark on a round of University interviews. I think I need to look serious and academic, so I buy myself a C&A plain pinafore dress and a white blouse. Aberystwyth is the most exciting interview, involving a three train journey each way and a walk down the front to see the sea. Leicester, Nottingham and Warwick are just days out. I receive offers from all – the arrival of these letters is very exciting – and I choose Leicester because they make the lowest offer, Nottingham in reserve, and like all the KEGSH girls, I am very humble. The teachers are very low key in their praise.

"Also," says Mom, "if your Dad has got to take and bring you back, we don't want him driving all over the country." "There's a Midland Red Service between Brum and Leicester and Nottingham too," says Dad, "if she wants to come home at the weekend."

Now all we have to do is pass our A Levels and finish School. In fact, we finished most of our set texts last year and are now embarked on revision and past papers, except when Mrs Gough panics as we have spent so much time on Wilfred Owen that we have to rush through *The Return of the Native*. It's common for us to come into school and say we had nightmares in which we sat the exams having done no work at all, but School takes all this very calmly and does not encourage us to panic.

Shortly before the A Levels, with extreme sadness, I hand in my notice at the Library and finish my half-baked romance with Digger. I need to focus. Had I been offered a full-time job, had I had a boyfriend that I cared about, I might have stayed at home; in such ways is our future decided. My friend

Lynne Atkins is not going to university, she has a boyfriend, Keith, and she wants to stay with him. They've been married over forty years now.

I am eighteen in February 1975, the first of my group to celebrate my eighteenth birthday, and we head out to Fanny's, where I legally and with some distaste quaff a Barley Wine while the girls look on enviously as they nurse their Britvic oranges and tonic waters. Barley Wine is pretty ghastly and is soon ditched for Woodpecker cider.

"I can vote now," I say confidently. "I'm Labour, like Mom and Dad." Lorna also expresses this view, whereas Yvonne turns out to be so radical, we decide to dub her Little Commie. My parents and all their friends get together to get me a silver charm bracelet from the Jewellery Quarter, very fashionable at this time, with a charm from all of Mom and Dad's friends, the Atkinses, the Bowmans, the Styles, the McManuses, the Grogans and my dear Uncle Albert and Auntie Mary.

"So you can remember all of us when you are gone," explains Mom.

I have it still – it reminds me of all of them, who are now all gone.

The Exams take place in the same atmosphere of calm that the school promotes: no shrieking, no hysterics, no fainting. The larger groups are in the Hall, facing the great wooden clock, but the majority are in the Sixth Form block, supervised by calm teachers. I sit through the Latin papers alone as Miss Boggis gazes on serenely.

Rather annoyingly, the school exams coincide with my cousin David's wedding to Marian at the Birmingham Registry Office, followed by a Reception at the Rep and I'm cross about that because the New Rep is one of my favourite places.

The Exams wind slowly down and we are sent off to do Community Service. Mine is at Dudley Road Hospital, a journey on the circle bus and where I make beds and serve tea all day and decide that I do not want to be a nurse.

We miss Sports Day, the Swimming Gala and the Flower Show, but are invited back for the Last Day. It is a sad day, with a final assembly, a final singing of the school hymn, a final saying of the Founder's Prayer and we walk out for the last time to the strains of Mrs Geoghegan (Music) playing Mozart's *A Turkish Rondo*. We say tearful farewells in the Sixth Form block, take photos, and sign each other's autograph books. I take around my copy of the school magazine *The Beacon* for signing, in which my final publication, *Ode to a Telegraph Pole* appears; I wrote it gazing out of the window, while I was bored.

"But maybe you could write a piece on your early days at university for next year's edition," smiles Mrs Davies.

School finishes at lunch time; we walk out for the final time and on Rose Hill Road, I stand and look back at the beautiful red brick building which has been a part of my life for seven years. It done good by me. It gave me values I treasure to this day: care, compassion, charity, humanity, tolerance and understanding. It taught me the meaning of hard work and the value of education. It taught me stoicism and endurance. It showed me that women could have a career. That we could do or be anything. That a community could live together in peace, in tolerance and diversity, whether Catholic or Protestant, Hindu, Sikh or Muslim, English, Welsh, Scots, Irish, Greek, Italian, Polish et al. Devoted to a common good.

I gaze at the school badge, the lion and the unicorn, rampant over the front door, the mottos: *Dieu et Mon Droit. Honi soit qui mal y Pense* – shame on him who thinks ill of it.

There now embarks a period of limbo while I wait for my results. Dad has filled in my grant application for Birmingham City Council; when the letter arrives, he is annoyed to find out my grant is reduced because Mom works. However, after payment of residence fees (tuition is paid directly), I will have £4.00 a week left which seems a great deal and maybe I can get back at Littlewood's over the holidays. I think of Julie and Mrs Randle, ecstatic to see me back, but on the negative side, the dreariness of the ladies' bloomers counter. Possibly at Christmas, it might get a bit festive and offer red bloomers with sprigs of holly embroidered on them, which might be a bit jollier. And play Slade singing *Merry Xmas Everybody* over the tannoy.

In the meantime, as I am economically inactive, I read the job vacancies board outside Dillon's the Newsagent in the Precinct, and end up with a summer job dolefully filling shelves at Sainsbury's right opposite. I realise I will always have to *work*. That I can never do *nothing*. Susie chatters excitedly about her new job at Birchfield Library, which makes me nostalgic for something better.

"When you catch the bus there, don't walk under the underpass, cross at the lights," dictates Mom. This is because the much vaunted underpasses of the redevelopment are now regarded as smelly, and indeed rather dangerous, places.

Dad has been talking for some years about buying New John Street West under the Right to Buy. His friends, Johnnie Murray, Johnnie Bowman, Stan Atkins, are telling him not to, to buy in Great Barr or Sutton Coldfield. Nobody buys houses on the Newtown Estate; you buy, if you get a mortgage, up the road in Perry Barr. But we know why Dad can't. It's Mom. She thinks the house is haunted by Nan and she swears that every day as she walks Sarah the Dog past Fallows House, that she hears Nan calling. And in later years, she won't leave because she thinks Dad haunts it. And after she dies there, I walk round the house, and yes, I can feel they are there, but I see nothing and within a few days, there is nothing there at all. Just absence. Not presence.

In the meantime, Dad wants to be a homeowner like Johnnie Murray with Maureen and Paul and Ann-Marie in Perry Barr, or the Atkinses with Lynne and Andrew in Sutton Coldfield, or all the others in Great Barr. So he goes to the Council. The house is worth £11,000, they explain and he has paid so much rent that he can have it for £2,000. "Why, I've got that in the Building Society," says Dad, surprised.

After filling in all the paperwork, he goes up to the Halifax on Colmore Row and draws out £2,000 in cash which he takes up to Bush House. He is now a home owner and many years later, when we sell the house after they are gone, I find all these typewritten records.

Apart from shelf stacking in Sainsbury's I spend the summer playing Buckaroo, Kerplunk, Cluedo and Monopoly with Susie and Kim in the garden, under Dad's laburnum tree. There is one more family holiday at Perran Sands, but it's a disappointment to me as Lynne isn't coming; she wants to spend time with Keith. Because I don't want to sit in the bar with the grown-ups, drinking Woodpecker cider, I spend my time in the playroom with the young Styleses, Sue and Harold, Andrew Atkins, and Helen and Lisa McManus. Roy McManus, Mom and Dad's friend, invariably called Mac, married Doreen later in life much to my disappointment, as I thought he was waiting for me to grow up.

All these children are lovely, but I do reflect that I need to move on – to drink with friends of my own age.

Most daring of all is a coach holiday that Lorna, Janet, Yvonne, Kerry and I book in Grange over Sands. This is our first holiday without our parents. We book the caravan through the *Evening Mail* and the coach at Digbeth, and enjoy glorious weather and the beauty of the Lake District. In the evenings, we drink cider legally at the local pub.

A Level Day is in August and Sainsbury's allows me a day off to go up to School for my results. In order to show my grown up credentials, I lounge into Miss Sargeant's office in jeans and a cheesecloth top, platform cork heeled sandals and my sheepskin collared suedette coat. She eyes these with disdain, as she also does my recently lightly permed hair (never allowed at school and not really successful, done with a Toni home perm kit).

"Ah yes, Grace... your results weren't too bad. Oh yes," and she glances at a list. "A for English, A for French and A for Latin. Well done."

I am speechless. All that study, all those years leading up to this moment. The first ever family member to go to University. Thanks to a Council grant. And KEGSH.

I am ready to go.

My daily walks to Sainsbury's in the Precinct, the discussion over the house buying, show me how the estate is deteriorating. Cracks are beginning to appear in the concrete of the high rises. The staircases smell. People who can buy are getting out to Perry Barr, Erdington and Great Barr. They are replaced with what the Council euphemistically calls "problem families". The playgrounds are full of rubbish. The new pubs are now, Dad says diplomatically, becoming "a bit dangerous to drink in". There are rumours of drugs on the estate. Although the Reverend Geoffrey Brown's successor, John Cox, does his best, the Church is now shut and empty much of the time. Events such as the Bonanza are over. The Brownies no longer meet at the Settlement. And the shops are closing down one by one in the precinct, the banks the first to go. The market is an almost empty shell. Factories are closing down or moving – the Crocodile Works, Brandauer, Box Carton, Newey's. The estate began with such promise, like the Seventies, that angry decade full of strikes and strife. I do not know when it lost its heart and soul. When the Council estates which were built to give us somewhere fit to live in became such a problem. The Newtown estate is still there, but now even the swimming baths and Community Centre are closed.

I fill in an application form for residence at Leicester, asking for a single room and I am awarded a room in somewhere called Herrick House. Disappointingly, it is an all-female residence. I seem fated to be with the girls. There is an Open Day one Saturday at the campus and we all go over in the car, still the much hated A60. The library, we are informed, is the oldest building on site and was once the County Asylum. Much more interesting to me is the English Department in the Attenborough Building (named for Leicester's most famous family), as this tower block has a paternoster lift which Mom and Dad adamantly refuse to try, but Susie and I ride all the way to the top and over and under the bottom.

This is followed by the excitement of Susie's O level results. She gets what she wants, but enters the Sixth Form reluctantly. "I think I'll just look for a job in the library service," she says. But when she goes back in September, I hear her tales of Sixth Form life wistfully. It is over for me.

I spend my Sainsbury's money on clothes which I feel suitable for student life, eyeing up the students in town. With relief, I hand in my notice at Sainsbury's. There's a final, teary farewell night with Lorna, Janet, Yvonne and Kerry at Fanny's in Birmingham (we can all now drink Woodpecker cider legally), and a trip to the library to return all the books which were on the First Year Reading List sent to me by Leicester University Department of English.

One fine Saturday morning at the end of September, we put my clothes, books, records, newly acquired stationery, transistor radio and the Dansette into the car, which makes it rather crowded as Susie, Sarah the Dog and Floss are coming too. "I think the car's sagging at the rear," says Dad, worried. We head out down Newtown Row to the Middleway and left onto the Expressway towards the M6. I look left and right, at Aston Church, Aston Hall, the park. I am leaving Birmingham. I am leaving home. I am excited, but also sick with nerves.

We draw up over an hour later at Herrick House, which is situated at College Hall, an area of Leicester known as Knighton. The Queens Road, which faces it, leads right up to the University, which is in the middle of Victoria Park. "Lots of shops, anyway," says Mom.

Herrick House's Warden sends me up to College Hall Reception for my keys. Reception is full of very young and very nervous looking students. We are told to go up to the University tomorrow to pick up our grant cheques (I panic, I don't know where the nearest Lloyds Bank is, how do you find out?), and for Department inductions. And that there's a Welcome Evening for all new students in the College Hall Bar after dinner tonight (I brighten, boys and drink). I'm standing with two girls also waiting for Herrick; one has curly dark hair and the other long, black hair. They introduce themselves as Anne and Jane. I'm aware that once again I need new friends. But they disappear upstairs when we get back. Maybe I'll see them in the bar.

Susie has drifted off to wander around the grounds, which are in fact really lovely, with Sarah the Dog and Floss has gone with her. The day is bright and sunny for late September and full of promise. At the door of Herrick One, a bedroom on the ground floor, Mom and Dad are excitedly talking to a couple of their age. "You'll never guess what, Grace, there's been a mistake! You're sharing with Angela and these are Sean and Betty, her mom and dad, and they've come all the way from Crawley!"

My heart sinks with a thud. I haven't shared a room for six years. But Mom and Dad are ecstatic because Sean and Betty remind them of all their Irish friends. They chatter excitedly away as I sulkily heave the Dansette into Herrick One. Sean, I hear, is a chef for the NHS and he's been here since he joined the RAF during the war, and Betty works for Trusthouse Forte and is a shop steward (Mom pricks up her ears). I hear Sean say, "We were worried about Ange, we thought it'd be all the middle class kids here, but it'll be grand for her to have Grace as a friend, we're just like each other!"

I open the door and go in. A tall girl, with light brown hair and dressed in what seems to me to be very fashionable clothes, swings round. I stop dead. She has a fag hanging from her lipsticked mouth. I hear Betty's soft Irish voice behind the door.

"And Ange doesn't know we know she smokes in the bathroom, but we do, and she tries to blow it out the window. Grace will just have to ask her to stop."

Instead, Ange wordlessly offers me a Benson and Hedges. I shake my head, also wordlessly, but tempted.

After unloading the car, there is a very bad moment when we have to wave our families off (I'm in tears over Sarah the Dog, Susie is in tears over me), and then we eye each other up, sitting gingerly opposite each other on our narrow beds. We do what the British and Irish always do.

"Let's put the kettle on and have a cup of tea," I say.

It was the start of a friendship that has lasted nearly fifty years.

*   *   *

I never really lived in Birmingham again. I went home for the holidays and spent a brief period there in the late 1980s, but from now on I would live in Leicester, Loughborough, Nottingham, the USA, Stourbridge and Wales. Mom and Nan only ever had three addresses each, all in Birmingham, all their lives; I have had so many, all over the world, that my friends' address books are full of crossings out under my name. But Birmingham made me. It was my city and I never really left. I was a child of two council estates, the Back to Backs, two council houses, two state schools, the working classes, the Welfare State, the Council, the NHS. And I was A Grammar School Girl.

Bibliography

Armstrong, Eric. *Old Handsworth, Lozells, Birchfield and Perry Barr* (1999).

Douglas, Alton. *Birmingham Back to the Seventies* (2007).

Douglas, Alton. *Birmingham in the Seventies and Eighties* (2013).

Douglas, Alton. *Birmingham in the Seventies* (2001).

Drake, Peter, and Jon Glasby. *Newtown and Summer Lane (Images of England)* (2006).

Edwards, Fiona, and Lewis, Brian (eds). *Talk about Newtown* (1992).

Tait, Derek. *A 1970s Childhood: From Glam Rock to Happy Days* (2011).

Thorne, Alison (Mrs Thorne, History). *King Edward's Grammar School for Girls, Handsworth 1883–1983* (1986).

Wager, A. *A History of King Edward VI Handsworth School 1983-2011* (2012).

Various past editions of the KEGSH School Magazine, *The Beacon*.

There are many books on the emotive subject of the Birmingham Bombings. I read Chris Mullin's *Hinterland* (2016) and *Error of Judgement* (1986).

The Justice for the 21 website is comprehensive and moving: *https://justice4the21.co.uk/*

And for who the Twenty-One were: *https://www.bbc.co.uk/news/uk-england-birmingham-47375087*

Also very useful were the BBC Four documentary *Birmingham Irish I am*, aired 2020, *Who Bombed Birmingham* (Granada TV, 1990) and *World in Action: The Birmingham Six, Their Own Story* (Granada TV, 1991). Also *The Reunion: the Birmingham Six*, aired on Radio Four in 2015.

The history of King Edward's Grammar School can be found on the website: *https://kingedwardvi.bham.sch.uk/about-us/history/*

The Radio Times online 1923–2009: *https://genome.ch.bbc.co.uk*

Thanks and Acknowledgements

Thanks to Ann Jolly, who set up the KEGSH Facebook page through which many of us were reunited and Paulette Burkill of the Old Girls Association.

And in memory of Ann Jolly, who died in 2022, and Margaret McLaney, 1968–1973, who died in 2021. Both of them one of us. Always.

'No Man is an Island'

No man is an island entire of itself; every man
is a piece of the continent, a part of the main;
if a clod be washed away by the sea, Europe
is the less, as well as if a promontory were, as
well as any manner of thy friends or of thine
own were; any man's death diminishes me,
because I am involved in mankind.
And therefore never send to know for whom
the bell tolls; it tolls for thee.

John Donne, 1572–1631

And any woman, too. Womankind. Any KEGSH girl.

Afterword – What Was Left

The Newtown Estate still stands in 2021 and the high rise blocks have undergone several refurbishments. The Precinct, which became increasingly empty and derelict, was eventually demolished and replaced by a smaller, newer complex. The Bartons Arms still stands, but The King of the Road, The Griffin and The Paddock have been demolished. All the Summer Lane pubs are closed, apart from The Barrel, still going strong. The Lamplighter survives as a church. Tucker Fasteners and Lucas's Great King Street have been demolished, though Lucas's Great Hampton Street survives as flats. The Newtown Palace, the Orient, the Villa Cross and the Aston Hippodrome were also demolished. St George's Church still stands in an empty Lucas's Recreation Ground. Brandauer's Factory and JC Newey are empty, but the Crocodile Works became housing, although only the facade remains. Spartan Steel is now a Royal Mail building. The Birmingham Settlement is still on Tower Street, but has moved to another building. The park in Tower Street is still there, but minus a playground and a parkie. Recently, Newtown Swimming Baths and Newtown Community Centre were closed down. Newtown Health Centre survives in an almost empty shopping precinct, now surrounded by a high fence. Sadly, the splendidly old fashioned White's Ironmongers on Summer Lane was demolished as late as 2022, to make way for flats.

Littlewood's closed down many years ago and the building in the City Centre is now Boots. Many of the rest of the shops in the City Centre of the 1970s have gone: Lewis's, Chelsea Girl, C&A, Grey's, Richard Shops, BHS, Woolworths, the Midland Educational, the Co-op, Hudson's Bookshop etc. Fanny's opposite Snow Hill is also gone, as is the Kardomah Coffee Bar, the Tennessee Pancake House and the Silver Blades Ice Rink. Snow Hill Station was demolished. The New Street Odeon is still there. The Queensway Odeon is closed, though surviving underground, a time capsule. The Gaumont and ABC Bristol Road are long demolished. The Kennedy Memorial mosaic was dismantled, but the remnants later reassembled in Digbeth. The atmospheric Old Rep still stands as an amateur venue.

Central Library, where I later returned to work as a professional librarian, was also demolished. Those of us who worked there have fond memories of what was then Europe's largest Reference Library. The staff, the resources, the collections, the ideals, the service, the community work, the facilities, were all excellent. We did not see it as a place which looked as if books were incinerated there. Like the Seventies, it began full of hope and like that sad decade, dwindled down into controversy, decay and recrimination. The concrete cracked and could not be repaired.

King Edward's Grammar School for Girls, Handsworth, which opened in 1911, is still flourishing in the same building and has an active Old Girls' Association, to which I still belong. I always belonged there. *Dieu et mon Droit.* Miss Boggis and Miss Naish recently celebrated their 100th birthdays and lived in the same sheltered housing complex, until 2022, when Miss Boggis passed away aged 101. *Vale, optima magistra.* Sadly, Miss Reid and Miss Sargeant have also passed away. Their photographs can still be found in the Hall.

Honi Soit qui mal y Pense.

By the Same Author

The Girl from Guildford Street, pb, 978-1-85858-579-6, £12.95
Tales of Guildford Street, pb, 978-1-85858-709-7, £8.95

Available from www.brewinbooks.com